M000213965

Reflections for the Call
A Devotional for Young Preachers

KYLE J. BOYER

RX2
PUBLISHING

REFLECTIONS FOR THE CALL by Kyle J. Boyer
Published by RX2 Publishing
Coatesville, PA 19320

Unless otherwise noted, all scripture quotations are from the New Revised Standard Version of the Bible. Copyright © 1989 by the Division of Christian Education of the National Council of the Churches of Christ in the United States of America. All rights reserved.

Scripture quotations marked KJV are from the King James Version of the Bible. Public domain.

Scripture quotations marked NIV are from the Holy Bible, New International Version®, NIV® Copyright © 1973, 1978, 1984, 2011 by Biblica, Inc.®. All rights reserved worldwide.

ISBN-13: 978-0999817506 (paperback)

To MY FAMILY,
who, no matter what, has believed in me, supported me, and walked with me, even when the endeavors seemed crazy. I love you, and hope every action I take reflects the foundation you've provided for me

Contents

Acknowledgments vii

Foreword ix

Introduction.. xii

Day 1 Study 1

Day 2 Be authentic 4

Day 3 Pray 7

Day 4 Have integrity 10

Day 5 Stay in your place 13

Day 6 Read 16

Day 7 Remain humble 19

Day 8 Wait... 22

Day 9 Be faithful to home 25

Day 10 Prioritize the anointing 28

Day 11 Never neglect family or friends...................................... 31

Day 12 Appreciate what you have 33

Day 13 Always have a mentor.. 36

Day 14 Learn from mistakes 39

Day 15 Progress in secular ventures 42

Day 16 Be relevant 45

Day 17 Practice... 48

Day 18 Be bold 51

Day 19 Be a servant.. 54

Day 20 Learn to hear God's voice 56

Day 21 Rely on the Holy Ghost 59

Day 22 Be self-aware.. 62

Day 23 Be true to the Gospel of Jesus Christ 64

Day 24 Be accountable to a pastor 67

Day 25 Never ask to preach 70

Day 26 Learn the discipline of consecration 73

Day 27 Love people... 76

Day 28 Feed the people 79

Day 29 Enjoy your youth 82

Day 30 Avoid the temptation to compare 85

Afterword 88

About the Author... 91

Acknowledgments

This book would not have been possible without the biblical foundation I received at the Mt. Carmel Church of God in Christ in West Chester, PA. For that reason, I must thank Pastor Milton E. Baxter, for his support in ministry and the many opportunities he has provided me. Those opportunities are reflected in the contents of this devotional. Also, thank you to Elder Bruce E. Hauser, whose support enabled the completion of this work. I would like to thank my professor and mentor in social justice work, Dr. Wayne E. Croft Sr., for his feedback. Dr. Marsha Brown-Woodard took the time to review the work, as did Dr. Chadwick Carlton, Dr. Timothy Fair, and several other classmates. I must appreciate Superintendent Linwood Dillard for his contribution, and for his support of young preachers. Lastly, thank you to my friends. Our conversations over the years have helped me think through the expressions that follow. To each of you, I am grateful. I am confident that as a result of your support, many young preachers will be strengthened in their call, and many souls will come to know the Lord Jesus Christ.

Foreword

"David served the purpose of God in his own generation."
—Acts 13:36, KJV

God has always raised up leaders and representatives from generation to generation who were responsible for impacting and influencing their respective space and time for his purposes. What is most intriguing though is not the purpose alone but the journey that God allowed them to take that led to the divine moment and call. From a biblical perspective, the journey is always one of preparation to ensure the proper stewardship of the call; an understanding of the weight and burden of the responsibility; the development of godly character; and the infusion of wisdom. Ultimately, wisdom is the principal thing, and it comes from God, the experiences He allows us to have, and people. That wisdom gives us knowledge, understanding, and a plan of action. Those who have been called to the ministry must first be partakers of the fruit of wisdom if they are to successfully fulfill the call of God on their life. Many times, it is not the preaching gift or ability that is the challenge, but it is the development and character of the preacher that may be compromised. In other words, the preacher's preaching does not always match the preacher. Gaining wisdom, then, is key.

Speaking of God allowing us to gain wisdom from people, wisdom from people can come through direct relationships, books they have written, or simply by observing their life. Often, I reflect upon the time I answered the call to the preaching ministry at the age of fifteen. I was so blessed to have my grandfather as my pastor and spiritual father who literally mentored and poured into me as a young, teenage preacher. He taught me so much regarding consecration, holy living, humility, servanthood, leadership, protocol and etiquette, loyalty, sanctification, faithfulness, and the list goes on and on. I came to appreciate and understand that these were the kinds of qualities that *really* made a great preacher. Other great leaders impacted my life in a very significant way. The vulnerability, innocence, lack of experience, ambition, and energy of the young preacher must be covered and directed. Many great preachers never reach their full potential and see the fulfillment of what God could do through them because of the lack of wisdom. In addition, I am thankful for my peers who were also aspiring ministers. I always sought friendships and connections I believed could make me better.

It is exciting to see the master plan of God continually fulfilled through young men and women whom He has chosen that have prepared themselves. It is a must that each preceding generation share essential qualities, principles, and wisdom nuggets with the next to ensure that the effective ministry of the preacher continues without reproach and shame. One of the most impactful tools for young preachers is peer mentoring and peer empowerment, as "Iron sharpens iron" (Proverbs 27:17). Many younger pastors, preachers, and leaders consistently reach out to me asking for mentorship. I am always excited to share my stories, journey, failures, successes, experiences, and principles to live by. Also, there are always inquiries about books and articles for a young leader I may recommend. Added to that list of recommended books is this devotional, *Reflections for the Call* by Elder Kyle J. Boyer.

Elder Boyer is a young, educated burgeoning minister of the Gospel, emerging community leader, and shining star. We are excited about what the future holds for him and what God will do through his life and ministry. He has been able to accomplish much in his personal life, career, and ministry. What a great balance! Now, Elder Boyer has authored this critical peer-to-peer presentation highlighting thirty practical ideals and principles for young preachers. I have no doubt this work will enlighten, enhance, educate, and empower the young preacher and prepare them for success in ministry, avoiding pitfalls and the traps of Satan. Always remember, your preparation will become someone else's garment for salvation and even progress. This book indeed is apt for this generation and will be an incredible resource for generations to come, as these principles are timeless.

Linwood Dillard
Pastor, Citadel of Deliverance, Memphis, TN
Chairman, COGIC International AIM Convention

Introduction

"Therefore, my beloved, be steadfast, immovable, always excelling in the work of the Lord, because you know that in the Lord your labor is not in vain."
—I Corinthians 15:58

Like so many other young preachers, I grew up practicing preaching. I am regularly reminded by childhood friends, childhood neighbors, babysitters, etc. that I demonstrated a call to preach as a child. I was a church kid, and like many church kids mimicking what I saw in church was second nature. There are stories for days, particularly the story of the cookout at my pastor's house when I climbed up on the jungle gym next door and preached to most of the members of my church. Looking back on those days, I'm no longer embarrassed, because I now understand the nature of purpose, destiny, and callings. No one is called to preach at the age of six, neither are they called to preach at the age of sixteen or fifty. God's callings are attached to our existence before we are conceived.

It was, however, at the age of sixteen that I finally accepted the call to preach. I had played around with the idea of preaching in my head for a little over a year, and for some time I kept asking God to show me signs if I was to really become a preacher. Each time the sign didn't manifest the way I wanted it to I would move the goalpost and ask him for some other indication. (I think I was doing that because I already knew that he wanted me to preach.) It was a Sunday afternoon in 2005 and I was outside getting ready to mow the lawn. (I should've done it Saturday but procrastinated.) I was in the middle of my teenage years, I had rededicated my life to Christ, and after realizing that I wanted to embrace a purer life, I found myself a little frustrated with church. I don't remember the exact nature of the frustration, but I felt like I wasn't giving my all to God.

At the time, we had a push mower at our home, and as the man of the house I was the designated mower. On this afternoon I was in the backyard preparing to mow, and I pulled the starter cord on the mower, but the mower wouldn't start. In the middle of my frustration, with church still on my mind, I paused and asked God, "Why do I feel like I'm not doing enough?" As loudly as I've ever heard God speak, the Holy Spirit plainly beckoned to my spirit, "Because you're not doing what I told you to do." It was the first time I remember receiving an immediate answer from God outside of an extended prayer time. To be standing at the edge of the backyard and hear God speak so plainly was new, but conclusive as well.

Of course, I knew what the Holy Spirit was referring to: God had already let me know I was supposed to preach. In the previous years several prophets had given me words, most of which I didn't understand or overlooked. During an altar call at a revival at my church a year or so before, Evangelist Janis Ruise told me, "You know you're marked!" I felt like I understood, but I overlooked that too. There were so many indications and confirmations that I could have embraced earlier. But I didn't because I wasn't ready. I, like many who will read and study from this devotional, ran from the clear call of God on my life, until I was ready to say yes.

Fast-forward more than a year, and on August 20, 2006, I delivered my initial sermon titled, "It's Not the Last Move," and the experience went well. Almost twelve years later, I can still preach that message, taken from Genesis 39:1-9, from memory. At the time, I was just starting out, and the expectations for how well I would preach during my first sermon were reasonable. Another benefit was that I even received a nice little offering, which was put to good use as I prepared to leave for college. I formally preached for the first time on that warm Sunday afternoon, and less than two weeks later found myself moving into my freshman dorm at the George Washington University. I remember it like yesterday, kneeling down in my prayer time at home on that Sunday evening, still riding a wave of excitement—I would later learn about the vulnerability of a preacher who has just poured out. In that prayer time, I heard something I'll never forget, "It won't always be like this." The Holy Spirit was letting me know that the preaching ministry would not always be easy, and of course, the Holy Spirit has proved true.

Today, young preachers face unique challenges, as we, unlike our more seasoned peers, have to balance the need to be proclaimers of the word, with all of the natural pressures that accompany youth. This devotional was born out of both experience and reflection. As I reflected I took the time to reach out to some of my many young preacher friends, both male and female, under the age of forty, who have at last five years of preaching experience. One of the greatest blessings of growing up in my denomination, the Church of God in Christ, is the many national gatherings we have, which provide a lot of opportunity for cross-pollination and sharing. There are some who argue that our organization has too many meetings, but one definite benefit of those frequent meetings is the frequent opportunity they provide to establish lifelong connections and friendship with other Christians from around the country, and indeed the world. Through those connections we gain brothers and sisters, we gain sounding boards, we learn about best practices, and we reflect on our own practice.

I have been able to preach from Joseph's story many times since that August 2006 day, and each time I continue to marvel at the wisdom of God's plan for Joseph. I often wonder what it would have been like had Joseph yielded to the pressures of his master's wife when she tried to force him into sleeping with her (Genesis 39:6-18). I often think to myself how different the storyline of the Old Testament would be if Joseph had taken the easy route, and given up in prison when it seemed as if God was no longer endorsing him. After all, Joseph did spend years in prison for a crime he didn't commit. I doubt I'm the only preacher to ever meditate on those issues, and I doubt I'm the only preacher, who, like young Joseph, has experienced moments of

DISAPPOINTED

YOU WON'T BE IF YOU WILL LET JESUS CHRIST BECOME THE LORD OF YOUR LIFE.

"For God so loved the world, that he gave his only begotten Son, that whosoever believeth in him should not perish, but have everlasting life. (John 3:16)

ASK JESUS CHRIST INTO YOUR LIFE AND YOU CAN HAVE PEACE AND JOY.

How can I become a Christian? Confess with your mouth and believe in your heart. (Romans 10:9-10)

You Are Loved!
Romans 5:8

JESUS IS LORD

You Are Loved!
1 John 4:9

immaturity, perhaps speaking out of turn. I doubt I'm the only preacher, who, like Joseph, had sufficient opportunity to give up when things got difficult. Surely, I'm not the only preacher to look around and wonder why God placed him or her in a particular position.

More will be said about Joseph at other points in this devotional, but one thing we should always remember about his story is that the story itself was part of God's plan. That is what I've learned to remember: I'm part of God's plan, as is every single soul I preach to. A plan implies intentionality and purpose. A plan implies a desired result and an expected outcome. If there is a well-designed plan for our ministry, which there is, it is our job to stick to the plan. With that in mind, we should endeavor to be, as the Apostle Paul wrote, "steadfast, immovable, always excelling in the work of the Lord" (I Corinthians 15:58).

As young preachers, part of being steadfast means being different. We are called to stand out via difference, yet our difference shouldn't overlook the mistakes that others have made. If there ever was a time when we needed to esteem certain values in preaching and reject others, it's now—there are some methods and practices in preaching that should be rejected, and we don't have to wait until we're advanced in age to reject them. The forces of hell are real, and want nothing more than to distort the perspective of a generation of proclaimers of the Gospel. Hell wants young preachers in particular to think that popularity and political influence are more important than souls and sanctification. Yes, even today, young preachers are still called to, as Paul told Timothy, "Preach the word; be prepared in season and out of season; correct, rebuke, and encourage," and we must do so "with great patience and careful instruction" (II Timothy 4:2, KJV).

However, to proclaim God's unadulterated truth effectively, we must proclaim it in a manner that is worthy of the message we proclaim. The world is looking at us, our peers are looking at us, and even the children below us are looking at us. We are responsible for the call of God on our lives. When we affirmed our acceptance of that call, it signaled that we accepted the job requirements that came with it.

As I spoke with some fellow young preachers about the advice they would offer to new preachers under the age of thirty in particular, there were some things that were almost universal, and some clear patterns that emerged. And yet, sometimes someone would offer a unique thought, or a perspective that I had never considered.

This devotional is perfect for new young preachers, particularly those under the age of thirty who are at the very beginning of their preaching journey, and are embarking upon preaching at an age younger than the age at which Jesus began his public ministry (thirty-three). The book is ideal for those for whom youth is still a major factor in ministry. Nevertheless, it is also of use to those who are over thirty. Some of the examples will resonate most with younger preachers, but all preachers can benefit from reflecting upon the advice, scriptures, and meditations that follow.

I hope that many pastors will choose to present young men or women a copy of this devotional as soon as they express a call to preach the Gospel. The devotional can probably be read in a few sittings, but it will be much more beneficial when embraced as a thirty-day journey, one day at a time. As you reflect upon the meditations, take the time to read the daily Bible readings, and use the accompanying prayers to guide your conversation with God. Take time to think about the work that lies ahead. Think about the ministry you are about to embark upon, and also think about the support you have been given.

I am confident that the one who enlisted us will always be there to help us—we can't leave him out of our ministries. My prayer is that if you are beginning your preaching journey, your time with this devotional will be a transformational experience, and that if you have been preaching for some time, this devotional will help reignite your passion for ministry.

Go forward, and preach in power, until souls are delivered, minds are set free, bodies are healed, the dead are raised, and communities are changed.

Kyle J. Boyer

"Now go, and I will be with your mouth and teach you what you are to speak."
—Exodus 4:12

Study

Blessed is the man that walketh not in the counsel of the ungodly,
nor standeth in the way of sinners, nor sitteth in the seat of the
scornful.
But his delight is in the law of the LORD; and in his law doth he
meditate day and night.
And he shall be like a tree planted by the rivers of water, that
bringeth forth his fruit in his season; his leaf also shall not wither; and
whatsoever he doeth shall prosper.
—Psalm 1:1-3, KJV

Daily Bible Reading: Psalm 1

By far, the advice given most by young preachers for other young
preachers is to study. It doesn't take long for preachers to recognize
the value of spending quality time in the word of God. There really is
no substitute for it. A preacher is called to proclaim the Gospel of Jesus
Christ, as expressed through God's word, and the only way to
effectively do that is to spend time studying, reviewing, and thinking
about the word.

Young preachers spend more time not preaching than they do
preaching. Knowing that, every young preacher is accountable for the
question, "What are you doing when you're not preaching?" The most
ineffective way for a preacher to study God's word is to wait until they
have to preach to study, especially the night before (or morning of).
Some people are phenomenal test takers, and can cram the night
before and still get an A. Most people do better with the alternative—

a regular plan of review and study. In my teaching career, I have often guided students through the development of good study habits, including notetaking, outlining, and creating flashcards, just to name a few. The secret is, each of those methods works for the study of God's word as well. You might still be a student at some level, so that example probably hits close to home.

Waiting until the night before you have to preach to open your Bible is the most ineffective way to take in his word. In fact, that is not study, that's rushing. Studying for messages should be easy, because you've already spent regular time in the Word of God.

The first psalm helps us understand this as well as any other passage of scripture. The psalmist is clear, those who delight in God's word—that means enjoy spending time in it—will find themselves planted and rooted. Not only will they be planted, but in the appropriate season they'll bear fruit. Those that do the opposite run the risk of not bearing fruit. Also, contrary to popular belief, it is possible to bear fruit in the wrong season, and when that happens we run the risk of our fruit spoiling, or others not valuing our fruit appropriately. The man or woman who meditates regularly on God's Word is planted in the right place, to bring forth fruit (success) at the right time—we can't beat that.

I've found in my journey that we sometimes focus too much on style, when substance is what matters most. Granted, style is important too, but the substance of preaching is what heals, delivers, and sets free. Style may excite, but substance empowers. Style may draw, but substance develops. While style succeeds only where the culture appreciates it, substance stands strong in every environment. Meaningful periods of study enable the substance of the word to work through our being first, further enabling us to preach with understanding and sincerity.

There is literally no other way to be effective than to make the basis of your ministry the word of God. Make a regular habit of reading God's word. But here is the key: don't just read God's word when it's time to preach. Find yourself in the word in season and out of season, find ways to apply what you read to your own life, and find ways to apply your life to what you read.

Figure out what works for you. You may find that you are able to listen to the word via audio track. Maybe it's convenient for you to follow a daily study plan. Maybe you are systematic and like to study one section at a time. Ask the Holy Spirit to lead you in the study of God's word, just make sure that you make a habit of studying.

Prayer: "God, your word is a light for my feet and a lamp for my path. I can only be effective in preaching if I'm able to study your word. If your word is hidden in my heart and recalled from my head, I can deliver it to your people with clarity. Bless me as I read and study your word; bless my eyes to read, my mind to receive, and my heart to retain, in Jesus's name. Amen."

Be authentic

"Before I formed you in the womb I knew you,
and before you were born I consecrated you;
I appointed you a prophet to the nations."
—Jeremiah 1:5

Daily Bible Reading: Jeremiah 1:4-19

Most people don't like fake things, and for good reason. A faux product doesn't have the same value as, and most of the time lacks the quality of, the real deal. The same can be said for the young preacher (and even the old preacher). The people want a real you, not a fake you. As a young minister of the Gospel, one of your chief aims should be authenticity.

In practice, authenticity means what we project in the pulpit should be a reflection of the real us. The contemporary problem is that today, we can access preaching at the click of a button. Years ago, preaching had to be studied from text, and students of preaching were forced to read the sermons they wanted to study. Later, audio technology allowed people to listen to sermons, and this made it easier for the mass production of homiletical styles. After that, video recording came around, and suddenly even mannerisms could be copied in a way they could not before. What is different today is that all of these means of "studying" preaching are accessible instantaneously. As a result, there is an ever-present temptation to try to be like other preachers. Avoid that temptation at all costs! Be yourself. People appreciate you, not you attempting to be something or someone you are not.

One of the most powerful responses of God to a young person in the Bible is the response he gave to the prophet Jeremiah in the days of Jeremiah's youth. This simple clap-back from God, directed to Jeremiah, teaches us everything we need to know about our existence. When Jeremiah's call was made known to him, Jeremiah questioned it, and argued with God. In the text, we see a young man (Jeremiah) reply to God with all of the reasons he felt he could not fulfill the assignment. God swiftly reminded Jeremiah that, even before conception took place in his mom's womb, he was known. Even more than reminding Jeremiah, God's response is a record for us. It is written in the word so that we are aware of the same fact regarding our existence. Just like Jeremiah, each and every one of us was known by God before our physical formation in our mother's womb. Not only did God know us before we were born, he even set us apart, and gave us preplanned assignments. At this very moment, each of us is walking out dates with destiny that were planned long before we ever thought about them.

If God knew us, and called us with specific assignments, surely, he wants us to walk in the identity he gave us. For that reason, we should have the strength to be authentic. After all, God formed us. He knew everything that he placed on our lives, and in our stories. No one wants to hear a carbon copy of someone else; they want to hear the vessel that's standing in front of them.

Be authentic, be real. Don't project something that is not there. It is in your authenticity that God can use you. It's like trying to fit a square peg in a round hole: it doesn't work, the cutout for the square only works with the square peg. Similarly, God gave you a message and a testimony. The Gospel given to you is only going to work through you. You have permission to be authentic.

Prayer: "God, in this age of YouTube, Facebook live, and instant video, it's tempting to try to be like others in the pulpit. I pray that you would strengthen me to be authentic, and to always be myself—the man or woman of God you have called me to be. Help me to appreciate who

I am, for even before I was formed in my mother's womb you knew me and ordained my purpose. Let my ministry be real. Let the word that I preach be the word that you've given through me, and not someone else. I ask this in Jesus's name. Amen."

Pray

In the morning, while it was still very dark, he got up and went out to
a deserted place, and there he prayed.
—Mark 1:35

Daily Bible Reading: Mark 1:35-39

It may come as a surprise to many that prayer is listed third, and not
first. There seems to be a prevailing assumption that if someone is a
preacher they regularly pray. It doesn't take long as a preacher to figure
out that is a false assumption. Far too many preachers neglect the
power and place of prayer, and eventually it shows up in a lack of
power in their preaching.

In *The Spirit of Python*, Pastor Jentezen Franklin wrote, "The most
powerful people on the face of this earth are those who have learned
how to pray. Not people who merely believe in prayer, or talk about
prayer, or those who can teach beautiful lessons on how to pray—but
people who take time to pray."[1] The sad truth is that prayer is often
the first convenient casualty of a busy life. It doesn't take much for the
preparation of a manuscript to suddenly seem more important than
prioritizing prayer. The slippery slope to prayerlessness begins with the
slick spot of laziness and the stumbling block of lack of discipline.

Prayer, like reading the word, is not something for us to do as a
result of being called to preach. We should pray because we desire a

---

[1] Jentezen Franklin, *The Spirit of Python: Exposing Satan's Plan to Squeeze the Life Out of
You* (Lake Mary, FL: Charisma House, 2013), 154.

close relationship with God. We should never be up to preach a message longer than we prayed about the message. We should never desire more time to proclaim the word than we desire to pray for a word.

Those truths fly in the face of what we often desire, especially since most of us glorify microphones. We also often glorify the amplification of our own voices. Yet, more than talking to or at a crowd of people, we must spend time talking with God.

Several times in the scriptures we find Jesus withdrawing to spend time praying. Immediately after we first meet him in his adult ministry, he is led into the wilderness where he spends time praying and fasting (Matthew 4, Luke 4). At the climax of his ministry, right before his crucifixion, he spends an evening in the Garden of Gethsemane praying (Matthew 26, Luke 22, Mark 14). In the first chapter of Mark, after dealing with intense crowds and the pressures of people, even the people he was ministering to, Jesus found that he needed to go to a deserted place and pray. Perhaps he needed to refill his spirit after pouring out, just like we need to do as preachers. Jesus was perfect and he had to pray. How much more, then, do we need to pray as imperfect people?

Communication between two individuals can involve discussion, debate, or dialogue. Too often in prayer we stay in the realm of discussion, simply feeding to God our desires in a one-way exchange. Debating with God is futile because he will always win, but when done right, prayer is a dialogue, a two-way exchange of communication. It's ludicrous to think that we can be instructed if our prayer life is absent of listening. In order to move in miracles, in order to move in not just declaration but demonstration, we have to talk with God in prayer on a regular basis. Talking with is better than talking to. In conversation with God there is an opportunity for him to pour back into us. Some of the best instruction comes from hymns, one of which says, "Have a little talk with Jesus, tell him all about your troubles. He'll hear our humble cry, and answer by and by." In prayer, God can only answer us if we give him a chance to.

Set up a regular time, both in the morning and in the evening. Maybe you're able to do longer prayers in the evening, and just a simple meditation in the morning, or vice versa. Whatever schedule or regimen God leads you to, stick with it. Know that you must have a prayer habit; there is no substitute for it.

Prayer: "God, you said in your word to pray without ceasing, and over and over you taught us the importance of prayer. I willingly admit that without constant communication with you, I cannot be an effective preacher. Help me to be consistent and strong in my devotional life. Help me to anchor myself in prayer—regular, meaningful prayer. I pray against laziness in my prayer life, I pray against inconsistency and lack of faith. Let my prayers avail much over the souls I preach to. Cause my prayer life to be effective and potent. Let the power of my prayer life be evident in every pulpit I mount. I ask this in Jesus's name. Amen."

Have integrity

"Now see to it that you drink no wine or other fermented drink and that you do not eat anything unclean. You will become pregnant and have a son whose head is never to be touched by a razor because the boy is to be a Nazirite, dedicated to God from the womb. He will take the lead in delivering Israel from the hands of the Philistines."
—Judges 13:4-5, KJV

Daily Bible Reading: Judges 13:1-5; 16:15-22

The dictionary defines *integrity* as "the quality of being honest and having strong moral principles" or alternatively "the state of being whole and undivided."[2] Let's take for a moment that second definition. We can think of integrity as not being divided between two representations of ourselves. One word conveys this well: *consistency.*

Every opportunity for service comes with a set of requirements and restrictions. There are certain things that police officers are not able to do; they are restricted from doing these things by law. Teachers in most public school districts across the United States can be fired for certain offenses like drunk driving or other drug-related offenses, even if the offense occurs outside of the classroom and off school premises. That's because jobs have particular requirements.

---

[2] *Oxford Dictionaries,* s.v. "Integrity," accessed December 1, 2017, https://en.oxforddictionaries.com/definition/integrity.

It is completely possible for us to live one life in public and another life in private, but we need to remember that living a double life will always catch up with us. One may be successful at it for a few moments, but never permanently. The Book of Revelation gives us a great example of this, as the writer describes the message for the church at Laodicea. The message was, "I know your works; you are neither cold nor hot. I wish that you were either cold or hot. So, because you are lukewarm, and neither cold nor hot, I am about to spit you out of my mouth" (Revelation 3:15-16).

Integrity is more than just consistency; it is also adhering to the job requirements even when people are not looking.

Samson was a Nazirite from birth. His mother was told that as a Nazirite he was to never indulge in alcohol, he wasn't allowed to touch unclean or dead things, and his hair was to never be cut (Judges 13:4-5). Those may have seemed like unfair requirements; however, for Sampson, they were the requirements. The only way that the power of God would be able to flow mightily through him would be if he followed those requirements. Unfortunately, Samson messed around and allowed an attractive woman (Delilah) to compel him to offer the secret to his power—the job requirements. Delilah used this secret against Samson, had his hair cut, and delivered him into the hands of his enemies the Philistines (Judges 16). In captivity, Samson suddenly found himself powerless.

I'm sure there are other scriptures that many would select before this one to teach a lesson on integrity, but I believe there is value in Samson's story for young preachers in particular. Preachers are called to be deliverers; that's one of the powers attached to anointed preaching: deliverance. However, there are job requirements that we must meet in order for deliverance to manifest.

There is a phrase I often repeat, "Live life in the light!" That means avoid dark places, hidden things, and secrets, which amount to the opposite of accountability, and constitute the breeding ground for sin. Sin loves darkness. In darkness habits can go unbroken, and demonic power can take root. Sin can't stand light. That's why it's so important to live our lives in ways that minimize darkness.

Quite frankly, nothing about the preaching ministry will prevent us from fornicating, and outside of the person one might fornicate with, no one has to know. Similarly, if we take enough preventative measures, we can engage in old habits just like we did before we were saved. However, let me caution you that lack of integrity (consistency, meeting the job requirements even when no one is looking) will catch up with you! Like Samson, we very well may jump up (or step up to preach) and realize that the power we once had is gone.

Don't fall for the trap of inconsistency. Live with integrity, and not because you were called to preach, but because as a Christian you honor the God that you committed to serve.

Prayer: "God, help my secret life to match my public life. Grant me the gift of consistency, and help me to live my life in the light. Help me to avoid the demonic power of dark places, and to walk with integrity. Just as you gave Samson job requirements, you have given them to me also. Help me to understand that my convictions are not those of my friends, but that the call of God on my life requires the restrictions you have given to me. I ask this in Jesus's name. Amen."

Stay in your place

And let us not be weary in well doing: for in due season we shall reap,
if we faint not.
—Galatians 6:9, KJV

Daily Bible Reading: Galatians 6:1-10

Being called to preach means that we believe that somebody called us,
and that person is God. Let's take a minute to follow that line of
thought. If one believes God called them, they believe he speaks. If
one believes he speaks, hopefully they can think of some promises or
declarations he has spoken over their life. That's the encouraging part,
God has made us promises! The problem for most of us is that there
is a wide gap between promise and performance of that promise. That
gap is called *process*.

In the middle of process, it's very tempting to want to go away from
where we're supposed to be. Sometimes as young preachers develop a
closer relationship with God, they are tempted to believe they suddenly
know more than the pastor. They may even prophetically see things in
the congregation and in the ministry, and it can sometimes cause zeal
and enthusiasm to overpower common sense. Avoid this temptation.

Every young preacher, and really every young person, has a place,
and that place should be in line with the leadership that they believe
God has assigned to them. Contrary to popular belief, we do have a
right to determine which leadership we submit to. Chances are if we
are under a leader who understands the call of God on our life and has

committed to helping us nurture that call, we are under the right leadership.

Over the years, I've heard the testimony of many young preachers who have made mistakes, and often, those mistakes were connected to being out of place. Of course, when we say *place*, we are not talking about a geographic location per se; we're speaking of positioning or posture—both mental and emotional. To grow as a preacher, we need to regularly ensure we are in the right place.

If your current assignment is to be the youth leader, which it very well may be, *that* is your assignment—not to be the senior pastor. One of the most quoted scriptures is Paul's powerful line to the Galatians. He essentially told them, "Don't be weary in doing what is right, because at the right time you're going to benefit if you don't faint" (Galatians 6:9). It is right to be in position, and wrong to be out of position. Therefore, Paul's message can be extended to say, "Don't be weary in staying in position."

Granted, this is one lesson that shows the importance of a prayer life. Being in position doesn't mean submitting ourselves to abuse. If God has led us to godly leadership, which he likely has, we should be confident in the leading of our pastor to place us in the appropriate position.

Stay in position, and be effective where you are. Don't allow the challenges of that assignment to cause you to abort that mission and drift to a place that you very well might not be suited for. If we stay in position, we will soon enough reap the benefits of all of the faithfulness and hard work that we have sown.

That is our mandate. We are called to be productive and be faithful to the place that we were assigned. In so doing, at the right time, we will reap. God has promised it.

Prayer: "God, you know how tempting it is to operate in areas other than the ones you have called me to. I pray that you help me to be in position. For each season, give me the ability to perform my duties where you expect me to be. Allow me to never find myself away from my post, derelict in my duty, or negligent regarding my responsibilities. Help me to avoid working in the wrong ministry, or accepting the wrong assignment. Help me to discern the right opportunities and the wrong ones, so that I may select the right ones and decline the wrong ones. I thank you for the grace to be in place, in Jesus's name. Amen."

Read

By wisdom a house is built,
and through understanding it is established;
through knowledge its rooms are filled
with rare and beautiful treasures.
—Proverbs 24:3-4, NIV

Daily Bible Reading: Proverbs 24:1-7

One of the beautiful things about Proverbs is the poetry that is used to describe very practical things in life. In Proverbs 24, the writer describes *wisdom* like a strong house, *understanding* as the way it is built, and *knowledge* as the beautiful furnishings that decorate it. Most of us want to live in a nice house, and we want to have a safe and sturdy structure with nice furniture to help us feel comfortable. If we want our preaching to be the same—that is, sturdy and safe and filled with beauty, we need to read.

It is fairly obvious to most preachers that they need to study the word, but it is much less obvious that in order to be relevant to the society we are preaching to, we also need to read things other than scripture. Without a doubt, many young preachers with some experience under their belt reference the need to read and read consistently as among the most important advice they could offer peers.

When we have a foundation rooted in the Holy Spirit, a prayer life that is strong, and a solid grounding in the word of God, we are led to literature and information that is beneficial for study. We should rest assured that the word of God is always applicable to life, but we need to have an understanding of life if we want to adequately apply the word to it. There is nothing wrong with consulting statistical data to back up what we reference in a sermon. There is nothing wrong with taking time to study Martin Luther King Jr., Saint Augustine, James Cone, or any of the other thousands of scholars and theologians both living and dead who can add to what it is that we have to say to people. Still, sermon preparation isn't everything. There is more to life than preparing messages, and reading is most important not for sermons, but for our own growth and development.

Trayvon Martin was only seventeen when his high-profile 2012 death helped spark a new movement for social justice in America. In 2017, his parents, Sybrina Fulton and Tracy Martin, co-wrote a book that tells their story and honors the legacy of their son. That book sits on one of my bookshelves now. It was hard to read Tracy Martin's description of his son, "Sometimes, I still see him, running across the public park football field, his shoulder pads too big for his slim frame, but his spirit large enough to make up the difference," and not be emotionally affected.[3] Unlike some of my other books this one isn't dense and complex like Augustine's *City of God*, neither is it a classic like Ralph Ellison's *Invisible Man*, but it taught me things about Trayvon Martin and his parents that I never knew. In other words, it helped me learn some things, and to learn is to gain.

There are seasons of our lives and ministries in which God leads us to certain types of texts. I've often been amazed at what I discovered while reading. Billions of people have walked the Earth, and we run the risk of missing out on some of their important stories if we fail to open up books. Information is now presented in myriad ways. With technological advances, we can choose from sources found in paper books, e-books, magazines, blogs, scholarly journals, and more. The key is to seek out that information and make time to take it in.

---

[3] Sybrina Fulton and Tracy Martin, *Rest in Power: The Enduring Life of Trayvon Martin* (New York: Spiegel & Grau, 2017), 18.

The writer of Proverbs 24 might not have been speaking of books purchased from Amazon or Barnes & Noble, but surely they were talking about wisdom and knowledge, the kinds of things that come from reading. Ask God to give you the ability to sit down and read. Make time to even read for fun. Find books that interest you, and substitute time in front of the television or on social media for time in a book. Doing so will not only support your preaching, but it will also expand your knowledge.

Prayer: "God, you've given us libraries, Google, and access to instant information. I pray against the spirit of laziness that would settle for scripture only. Show me and lead me to the scholarly resources and relevant information that can support my preaching. Help me to find books and readings, and to appreciate the work of scholars like Martin Luther King, Saint Augustine, and others. Help me to read things that can advance the word I deliver to your people. Give me a hunger for study, a thirst for knowledge, and a passion for learning, in Jesus's name. Amen."

Remain humble

In the same way, you who are younger must accept the authority of
the elders. And all of you must clothe yourselves with humility in
your dealings with one another, for
"God opposes the proud,
but gives grace to the humble."
Humble yourselves therefore under the mighty hand of God, so that
he may exalt you in due time. Cast all your anxiety on him, because
he cares for you.
—I Peter 5:5-7

Daily Bible Reading: I Peter 5:1-11; Micah 6:8

As preachers, we have to know that people are watching us. The
preacher is a public ministry gift. The word is very clear in multiple
places: God opposes the proud, but he exalts the humble.

Humility is difficult, as it is not one of those things that one can
aspire to; we just have to do it and display it. God instructs his people
to humble themselves; the alternative is not something most of us
want. To have God humble us means that we are signing ourselves up
to experience incredible pressure, in whatever manner God chooses to
give it to us. One of the ways that God humbles people is through
traumatic events. Sometimes he uses difficulties and particular trials to
bring down the proud.

Of course, there is no guarantee that we will avoid those things in
life. In fact, we know that we are promised to have some of them—
even when we are living right. The psalmist wrote, "The righteous

person may have many troubles, but the Lord delivers him from them all" (Psalms 34:19, NIV). But we don't have to experience those things beyond what God intends for our story. When we humble ourselves—meaning, wait our turn, submit, recognize that we are not quite as good as we sometimes think we are—we give God room to elevate us.

In first Peter, we read about this whole humility thing in terms of younger people accepting the authority of the older people. The instruction is given to "humble yourselves under the mighty hand of God" (I Peter 5:6). If we do that, the scripture promises that he will exalt us in due time.

There's another relevant passage found in the sixth chapter of Micah. Here, the question is asked, what does the Lord require of us? This text is one of the clearest and most concise examples of the Bible giving us our requirements as children of God. The requirements are simple. We are told to "act justly, love kindness, and walk humbly with your God" (Micah 6:8, NIV). As preachers those are the things we need to do. In all of our actions, especially in our preaching, we should act justly. Our preaching should never be lacking in mercy, because God is mercy, or what we know as love.

Finally, and most importantly, in our own walk we are commanded to walk humbly with God. Humility does not mean timidity, neither does it mean weakness. However, a major cautionary note is to remember that if we are effective in preaching, we are going to receive something that works against humility—applause. We must never allow ourselves to become drunk from compliments. The same people who love our preaching one day, will critique it the next. It's best to find fulfillment in the fulfilling of our assignment, and not in the feeling that comes from the cheers of others.

Remember that humility is a state of recognition—the recognition that by ourselves we are not that great. We do need a God, the true and living God. He is the one who called us to preach, and he is the one that will exalt us if we first humble ourselves before him.

Prayer: "God, I'm not asking you to humble me. I ask that you remind me to humble myself! For your word tells me to do the humbling, and with your prompting I can humble myself. Remind me not to be puffed up, even when that is not my intention. Help me to never allow the high of compliments and applause to go to my head or drunken me. Show me how to act justly, to love mercy, and to most importantly, walk humbly with you. I ask this in Jesus's name. Amen."

Day 8
Wait

But they that wait upon the LORD shall renew their strength; they
shall mount up with wings as eagles; they shall run, and not be weary;
and they shall walk, and not faint.
—Isaiah 40:31, KJV

Daily Bible Reading: Isaiah 40:25-31

One of the hardest things for anyone to do, let alone a preacher, is to
wait. Waiting is made even more difficult when we look around and
see others seemingly progressing faster than us. It's at those moments
that we need to be reminded that God's timing is not subject to our
understanding.

We may know a good friend or associate who started preaching at
the same time as us, and all of a sudden, we look to the left or look to
the right and see that they have advanced in a different (faster) manner.
In those moments, consider that God works his miracles in the middle
of difference. We must continually embrace the need to wait. There is
no other way. To get outside of God's timing is one of the most
detrimental things we can do to our ministry.

One of the most famous passage of scripture is one found in the
40th chapter of Isaiah. We're told that at times even young people—
who should really have the most energy and vitality—will sometimes
grow weary. We're told that sometimes young men and women will
burn out because of exhaustion. But we are reassured in the scripture
that when we wait upon God, he renews our strength, he helps us to

do what eagles do, which is soar effortlessly. We can progress on our journey without fainting.

Waiting on God gives us the ability to do our work without tiring and burning out. There is no reason why a young preacher just starting out should be burnt out. A burnt-out preacher is an inefficient preacher. A burnt-out preacher is also one who can never operate in God's supernatural grace while in that state.

For some reason, it seems like waiting can cause us to feel alone. I've come to believe that it's not the waiting that brings feelings of loneliness, it's waiting for the wrong things or on the wrong person. Imagine someone waiting for the mail to arrive via their microwave. Certainly that would be an exercise in futility. Waiting for popcorn at the microwave makes sense. The mail, however, is most likely to arrive via the mailbox and the mailman. In his sermon "God Calls Us to Be Eagles" taken from Isaiah 40:27-31, Dr. William D. Watley addressed the feelings of loneliness that can accompany a season of waiting. Watley stated, "I know that sometimes it appears that we are stretched out by ourselves; however, no one who flies leaning and depending on God ever flies by oneself, for 'the eternal God is thy refuge, and underneath are the everlasting arms.'"[4] The key to waiting, especially waiting for ministry progression, is to do so trusting in the God who called us in the first place.

None of us will pretend that waiting is easy, because we know that it is not. It is very tempting to think that we know where we should be. But in those moments, we must reassure ourselves that God knows best. Spend time in his word observing how he moved in the lives of those he called. Seek to be in the right place at the right time, or what Dr. C. R. Oliver calls *en punto*.[5] Make sure you are in the position that God wants you to be. If so, when the time is right God will move you higher, he will elevate you, he will redeem the time, he will make your efforts worth it.

Don't get ahead of yourself even though you might feel like you're ready. Wait.

---

[4] Samuel D. Proctor and William D. Watley, "God Calls Us to Be Eagles," in *Sermons from the Black Pulpit* (Valley Forge, PA: Judson Press, 1984), 103.

[5] C. R. Oliver, *En Punto* (The Woodlands, TX: Zadok Publications, 2013), Kindle.

Prayer: "God, I need endurance to survive the difficulty of ministry as a preacher. I see others moving in different timing, and I am tempted like all people to move outside of your timing. Help me to make use of the patience you have already given me. Help me to wait for my time of elevation and promotion. Help me to appreciate the seasons of hiding, so I may thrive in the seasons of exposure. Help me to wait, in Jesus's name. Amen."

Be faithful to home

"His master replied, 'Well done, good and faithful servant! You have
been faithful with a few things; I will put you in charge of many
things. Come and share your master's happiness!'"
—Matthew 25:21, NIV

Daily Bible Reading: Matthew 25:14-30

The first assignment and first duty of a young preacher is to their local
house.

Young preachers are prone to sticking out in a crowd, especially if
they're effective in ministry. If you're like the typical young preacher,
people are going to begin calling you to come and preach, and you're
going to start receiving increasing numbers of opportunities.
Sometimes the opportunities will be platform services, where there are
multiple speakers—one should never expect to be paid for these
engagements.

At other times, people request a young preacher for youth Sundays
or weekend youth services, and maybe even some opportunities other
than youth Sunday. In general, people understand that a young
preacher is not a senior pastor, and that most young preachers don't
have regular preaching opportunities. Many of these opportunities will
also be different depending on the region one lives in. There are some
areas where there are fewer young preachers, and thus a higher demand
for the few that are around.

Regardless, each of us has a responsibility to be faithful to our local assembly; and never get it twisted, everyone needs a local assembly. Our first work is at the church where God planted us. We may feel led to an evangelistic ministry, but even in that calling, we should know the difference between evangelism and itinerancy. Evangelists are those who go out with a specific mandate to win souls; itinerants are those who have a moving ministry, often preaching to those who are already saved. They are not the same. Preaching continually to crowds of church people in different places is not an evangelistic ministry; it is an itinerant ministry.

Matthew records Jesus telling the parable of the bags of gold, most commonly known as the parable of the talents (Matthew 25:14-30). These were not talents as in musical ability or preaching gifts. They were talents as in the ancient measure of weight. Authorities differ on how many pounds a talent was, but I believe it could have been anywhere from 50 lbs. to upward of 100 lbs.

In the parable, several servants are given different amounts of gold as an initial investment, according to their ability. As such, there were different expectations for what would be produced from those investments. The more that was given, the more that was expected. Each of those individuals needed to be faithful to what the master had given them, and the end product should've reflected what they were able to do.

Today God is calling for the same from us, particularly in our ministries as preachers of the Gospel. We are to be faithful to what God has given us, and not chase after other things. As far as young preachers go, it means there will be some times when we have to turn down preaching engagements. There is nothing wrong with taking opportunities to preach. In fact, that is what young preachers should be doing. It is a large part of how God helps young preachers develop their gifts. At the same time, we should never neglect home.

Our first priority on a daily and weekly basis should be to support our home church and the vision that God has given to our leader. We should never expect to be successful in our ministry if we are not found working diligently in at least one of the ministries in our local church.

The number one place for our preaching and leadership skills to be developed is our local assembly.

When we neglect these things, we run the risk of being like the prodigal son, the central character in another parable Jesus told (Luke 15). That young man wanted to take his inheritance early, and ended up wasting it. At the end of the story he had to come back, repent, and humble himself to start over.

We can avoid that by simply being faithful at home the first time.

Prayer: "God, you know how tempting it is to go wayward. Help me to never be like the prodigal son, who wandered away from home chasing fool's gold, only to have to humble himself and return. Allow me to be faithful to the vineyard and shepherd you've assigned for me. Help me to understand the importance of serving my home church first, and to be stable in my ministry. I thank you for stability, and faithfulness, in Jesus's name. Amen."

Prioritize the anointing

The Spirit of the Lord is upon me, because he hath anointed me to
preach the Gospel to the poor; he hath sent me to heal the
brokenhearted, to preach deliverance to the captives, and recovering
of sight to the blind, to set at liberty them that are bruised,
To preach the acceptable year of the Lord.
—Luke 4:18-19, KJV

Daily Bible Reading: Luke 4:16-30

When talking about the anointing in Pentecostal churches, we often
think of a scripture in the 10th chapter of Isaiah, in which we read that
the anointing destroys the yolk. It says that in the King James version.
Unfortunately, there is considerable debate about what that scripture
really means. Other translations suggest that the scripture is often
taken out of context.

That highlights something each of us needs to do: wrestle with
scripture. Regardless of the full meaning of that text, what we do know
from multiple examples in the Bible is that the anointing represents the
gift of God's supernatural approval and ability. As an action, the
anointing of an individual was done by pouring oil on their head to
represent God selecting them for a particular assignment. There are
plenty of examples of this, going back to when Moses anointed Aaron
and his sons as part of their induction into the priesthood (Leviticus
8).

Similarly, there was the anointing of objects for use in the temple. Probably one of the most famous instances of anointing someone is when Samuel poured oil on the head of David after the oil would not flow for David's seven older brothers (I Samuel 16). That is always a good reminder that God does not necessarily use the people humanity deems to be "most fit." In fact, in that same chapter of I Samuel, God had to remind the prophet that, "The Lord does not see as mortals see; they look on the outward appearance, but the Lord looks on the heart" (v. 7). God wants to anoint those whose hearts are correctly positioned.

We need the anointing; it is God's sanction, God's authority, God's blessing to do his bidding in our preaching ministry. We can tell, even if we can't accurately describe it in academic terms, the difference between those who are anointed and those who are not. The anointing makes a difference, it makes things happen, it causes us to be effective; that's why we need it.

There is a major difference between a cop who only carries a baton and a cop with a lethal weapon. The anointing is our power, it gives us an energetic charge in our work. And it is for that reason that we must prioritize it.

It is recorded in Luke that when Jesus got up to teach in the synagogue, he quoted from a well-known passage of scripture in Isaiah 61. Jesus said, "The Spirit of the Lord is upon me, for he has anointed me to preach the Gospel to the poor, to heal the brokenhearted, preach deliverance to the captives, recovery of site to the blind, and to set at liberty those that are bruised" (Luke 4:18).

That is what the anointing does. When one is anointed, it brings freedom and liberty to those who are captive and bound in any life situation. The Gospel, even though it's presented one way, ought to affect the lives of all of those who hear it preached on an individual basis. The anointing in our preaching is what allows us to stand up in front of a crowd of hundreds of people with different needs and different circumstances and reach them all on an individual basis.

We are to be agents of not just declaration, but also demonstration. We can only be that with the anointing. For that reason, we must prioritize the anointing.

Prayer: "God, even as Jesus was anointed to preach the Gospel, you have anointed me. I ask that you help me to prioritize the anointing. Help me to understand and recognize the cost and weight of the anointing. When I find myself under pressure, help me to, with the help of your Holy Spirit, seek the anointing more than popularity or anything else. I recognize that the enemy is after my anointing, but I affirm my belief in your power over the powers of hell. I declare my faith in your ability to help me to stand against the wiles of the devil, and to preserve the anointing that you have poured upon my life. Let my preaching heal the brokenhearted, deliver the captives, recover the sight of those living blindly, and give liberty to the bruised. I ask these things in Jesus's name. Amen."

Never neglect family or friends

And whoever does not provide for relatives, and especially for family members, has denied the faith and is worse than an unbeliever.
—I Timothy 5:8

Daily Bible Reading: I Timothy 5:1-8

Our service and time as a young preacher is preparation for the things God wants to do through us later. For many of us that will mean pastoral ministry, but for some of us, pastoring is not in our future. It is important that we understand that not everyone called to preach is called to pastor. Countless hours and resources have been wasted by those who, in error, have sought after the pastorate when that was never God's intention for their lives.

How we spend our time as a young preacher will have enormous bearing on our life later on. In many ways, young preachers are practicing for the future.

You may already be married, even in your young age. You may even have a family of your own, but if you are like most young preachers, you are not yet married and likely don't have any children. Whatever your personal life situation, your ministry should especially be a benefit to your unsaved friends. Those closest to us who haven't yet embraced salvation should be able to witness salvation through our lives.

I believe there should be some unsaved people in our life, because if not, we are not reaching any lost souls. There is nothing extraordinary about just preaching to saved people. In fact, it should be our life's walk that expresses Christ before we ever open our mouths. You may be working full time, and if that is the case, your life ought to express Christ on your job. It's usually a big clue that something in our ministry is wrong when no one outside of church culture is interested in our faith and ministry. We ought to get some questions and some interest in our salvation from those who are not saved.

That brings us to family and friends. We must make sure that we do not neglect them. There is a biblical mandate to appreciate and support our natural family. Similarly, it is on us to make sure we have a circle of friends that we can rely upon and trust when ministry in public becomes difficult. I was fortunate enough to befriend and grow with a group of other young preachers. Looking back, I can't imagine how I would've made it in ministry without some peers to share the experience. I am a much better preacher and man because of the many hours of fellowship, food, and fun I spent with my friends. Many of our decisions were made in counsel. We continue to work in ministry together, strategize together, bounce message ideas off each other, and again, have fun.

Never neglect family and friends. The Bible is very clear that those who do are worse than unbelievers. At least three times in Proverbs we read that "in a multitude of counselors there is safety" (Proverbs 11:14; 15:22; 24:6, KJV). None of us was meant to be alone all the time. We have a family—we wouldn't exist if we didn't have one. We are responsible for a crew of friends. We need them both.

Ask God to assist you in this area. Connections matter; be discerning in establishing them.

Prayer: "God, I don't want to fall into the trap of being so focused on preaching to your people that I forget my family and friends. Help me to discern the relationships around me, to love my family unconditionally, and to be connected with destiny friends. Help me to establish healthy and godly relationships that add to the quality of my life and support my ministry. Help me to never neglect family and friends, and to do so with balance. I ask this in Jesus's name. Amen."

Appreciate what you have

God sent me before you to preserve for you a remnant on earth, and to keep alive for you many survivors. So it was not you who sent me here, but God; he has made me a father to Pharaoh, and lord of all his house and ruler over all the land of Egypt.
—Genesis 45:7-8, KJV

Daily Bible Reading: Genesis 45:1-15

As a young preacher, it's easy to fall into something that I like to call "the plight of the wandering eyes." This is the problem that arises when we begin to think less of what God has given us and more of what he's given others, as a result of our gazing too much upon others.

God has already given each of us some things in our young ministries. The fact that we are at this point—having acknowledged calls to the preaching ministry—means that God has already spoken to us about some of the things he intends for our lives. When we consider what he has given us in the form of blessings in the present—perhaps material possessions and a small degree of wealth, perhaps much knowledge already, and especially godly relationships—all of these things should be considered valuable, and important to our ministries. Each of these things should also support our preaching.

There is a song that says, "Count your blessings, name them one by one, count your blessings, see what God has done." Far too many of us neglect to count, and thus be accountable for, our blessings. Sometimes there is an increasing temptation to look and to feel insecure about what we have, but God has already given us many blessings, and together they should work to make us better preachers. When we take inventory of those blessings regularly, it helps us stay in a mindset of gratefulness. Counting our blessings helps us give thanks to God for what he's already given us on a regular basis. We should continue giving God the glory for what we have, before we ask for more. Also, it is on us to make sure that we are being good stewards of what he's given us.

One of the most preached and studied stories in the Bible is the story of Joseph. Joseph's story, which dominates the latter part of Genesis beginning in the 37th chapter, is one that is key to the fulfillment of God's promise to Joseph's great-grand father Abraham. Abraham was promised by God that he would be the father of many nations, but there was a point when that promise seemed to be threatened by famine. Yet somehow, God provided deliverance for Abraham's grandson and great-grandsons. The story goes that even though Joseph had been sold into slavery by his jealous brothers, God's plan was put into place, and Joseph ended up becoming the number two in command of Egypt (Genesis 41:37-45). In that position, which many of us refer to as *prime minister*, Joseph was in a position to receive his family and provide food for them even in the midst of a severe famine. Joseph's family was preserved, and so too was the promise to Abraham.

Although more will be said about Joseph later in this devotional, for this, day 12, recognize the importance of Joseph's story as it relates to us understanding what God has given us. Joseph was a dreamer, and in his youth, he knew this, but was not mature enough to deal with it. God knew that Joseph lacked the maturity to handle his gifts, and God used Joseph's immaturity to prompt his brothers into jealousy. It all ended up working out for their benefit, but I'm sure they did not see that at the time.

The lesson for us is to recognize the value of the gifts God has given us. To many people, these gifts will appear offensive or off-putting. Many people will be uncomfortable with the gifts God has given us. Sometimes we will be uncomfortable with them. However, if we are going to be effective in the preaching ministry, it's important that we take inventory of our blessings and gifts. Greatness won't come to our preaching ministry if we neglect the ministry of gratefulness.

Prayer: "God, help me to avoid the plight of wandering eyes. I recognize that it's tempting to be ungrateful and to want what others have. I ask that you cause me to see the value of the things that you've already given me, whether it be possessions, knowledge, or relationships. Help me to take inventory of my blessings and even my talents. Before I seek to obtain other things, help me to understand what it is that I already have, and to appreciate why you've given it to me. I ask this in Jesus's name. Amen."

Always have a mentor

The glory of youths is their strength,
but the beauty of the aged is their gray hair.
—Proverbs 20:29

Daily Bible Reading: Proverbs 20:15-30

No one excels without mentorship in their life.

Mentorship should not be restricted to preaching. Everyone should have a mentor for every major thing they want to accomplish in life. If you want to be a carpenter, there should be a carpenter mentor in your life. If you want to progress as a teacher, you should have a teaching mentor. Likewise, in preaching, you must have mentorship, and there are many of us who have a mentor other than our pastor. To be clear, one's pastor can be, and often is, a great mentor. Just know that it is okay to have a preaching mentor who is not your pastor.

Mentorship is a form of impartation. There are some lessons that should be easier for us than they were for our mentors. There are some mistakes that mentors make that should not be repeated in mentees, because we have learned through them. Mentorship allows for the gleaning of experience from those who have already mastered what it is we are trying to accomplish.

Also, consider that mentors know more than we do and are able to pour that knowledge into us to advance our trajectory. They are able to check us when we go wayward, they are able to tell us honestly things about ourselves that we may not see. As far as preaching is concerned, a mentor can help us expand our preaching abilities, far beyond what we might be able to do otherwise. By the way, YouTube is not a mentor. It is imperative that we have a living, breathing mentor. Just never forget that the overall goal of having one is to increase effectiveness.

In an adult mentor-mentee relationship, the burden of initiating communication is on the mentee. It is not a mentor's obligation to reach out or offer assistance. However, the one caution is that we must always be prayerful in selecting a mentor. Mentors should never be abusive, verbally, emotionally, or otherwise. A mentor-mentee relationship is one that is professional. There should be clear boundaries, and an understanding as to the nature of the mentorship. It is important that any mentorship be under the counsel of a pastor. There should be nothing hidden about a mentor-mentee relationship.

Also, mentorships do not happen electronically! If your mentor does not know your name, and if you cannot call them on the phone or initiate one-on-one conversations, it is not a real mentorship. Period. In a mentorship teaching and instruction can certainly happen in a group format, but there must be opportunities for individualized learning and personalized feedback in order for the mentorship to be legitimate.

One of my favorite proverbs is found in the 20th chapter. The 29th verse suggests that the glory of young men is in their strength, and the beauty of old men is in their gray head. That scripture reveals to us that in youth there is a lot of strength, but wisdom comes with the experience of gray heads. Our strengths as young people require the wisdom of those who have gone before us. *Gray head* doesn't mean old; it means experienced.

If we truly want to advance in the preaching ministry, we must ensure that we have at least one strong preaching mentor who is willing to impart to us their knowledge and experience.

Prayer: "God, I thank you for surrounding me with people who know more than I do. Help me to always have a righteous mentor. Help me to discern those who are meant to pour into me, and those that I should avoid. Help me to glean from the expertise of those who have traveled the paths that I hope to travel. Provide for me preaching mentors who can show me the way to become more effective in the ministry that you have called me to. I thank you for these things, in Jesus's name. Amen."

Learn from mistakes

Not many of you should become teachers, my fellow believers,
because you know that we who teach will be judged more strictly. We
all stumble in many ways. Anyone who is never at fault in what they
say is perfect, able to keep their whole body in check.
—James 3:1-2, KJV

Daily Bible Reading: James 3:1-12

Jesus Christ was the only one to live a perfect life. He is the one we are
supposed to be preaching about. Outside of him, none of us is perfect,
and at some point, we are forced to acknowledge that. The beauty of
salvation in Jesus Christ is that we are not bound by our imperfections.
Acceptance of the call to the preaching ministry can sometimes put us
in the weird position of feeling inadequate. On the one hand, as
preachers we are seen in the public as having a higher level of
spirituality; on the other hand, we know the real us.

There are two kinds of mistakes: the mistakes that we make, and
the mistakes that others make. It is our responsibility to learn from
them all. It is on us to learn from our mistakes and not repeat them,
but we should also learn from the mistakes of others. There is no
reason that we should have to repeat mistakes that have already been
made.

The reference scripture in the third chapter of James reminds us
that, "Anyone who is never at fault in what they say is perfect, able to
keep the whole body in check," but before that, it is recorded that,

"We all stumble in many ways" (vv. 1-2). It's true, we are stumbling people. Although we do not have to make mistakes, our humanity will often catch up with us. The idea of this passage is not that there is a big group of people somewhere hidden who are never at fault—quite the opposite. The idea is that most people are at fault from time to time, and that we need to be aware of our own faults.

When considering mistakes, don't just think about the big ones. Waiting until the last minute to prepare a message might not be a "fall," but it is certainly a mistake. It only takes one or two instances of that happening for us to see the difference between preaching under those circumstances and preaching when we've spent enough time preparing. From that mistake, one should learn how much time they need to adequately prepare messages, and they should make every effort to set aside that amount of time going forward.

Similarly, saying something wrong from the pulpit is a mistake, but not one that we should beat ourselves up over—just learn from it. There is a lot of benefit to listening to tapes or watching videos of ourselves. Although it may feel awkward, it is one of the best ways to critique our craft, and ultimately improve our ministry. Listening to or watching ourselves allows us to realize our quirks, nervous ticks, repeated words, etc. Learn from those things.

Most importantly, take the feedback of others when you make a mistake, be open to receiving that feedback, and don't make the same mistake twice if you don't have to.

Recognize that God is bigger than our imperfections. God is able to help us be resilient, even past mistakes. God is so awesome that he can even use our mistakes to our benefit. Our faith in that assurance is what allows us to keep going even when we slip up or make an error.

Ask God to assist you beyond your shortcomings and failings. Ask God to help you recognize, and never repeat, the shortcomings and failures of yourselves and others.

Prayer: "God, I thank you for being bigger than my imperfections so that I don't have to repeat the mistakes of the past or the mistakes that I will make in the future. Help me to have the spirit of resiliency and the gift of grit. Help me to learn from my failings and shortcomings.

When I make an error, help me to get back up and not repeat what I did wrong. I thank you for the ability to overcome the moments when I miss the goalpost. I ask this in Jesus's name. Amen."

Day 15
Progress in secular ventures

And Pharaoh said to Joseph, "See, I have set you over all the land of
Egypt."
—Gen 41:41

Daily Bible Reading: Genesis 41:37-57

Church is more than a building; it is the body of Christ, and it is
ineffective if it is confined to a building. God called us to be the light
of the world, and he told us to let our light so shine before men that
they would see the good that we do, and end up glorifying our father
who is in heaven (Matthew 5:14-16). That lets us know that God is
even glorified by our success in secular ventures.

Sometimes as young preachers we think that the preaching
microphone is everything, when in reality our ministry is so much
more. Everything we do is ministry, whether we are a nurse, a teacher,
or even in our position as students—it is all ministry!

The story of Joseph continues to be instructive for young people in
ministry. After Pharaoh, who, mind you, was a secular king, revealed
that he had dreamed a pair of dreams, he was informed that there was
a young man in his prison who had the gift of interpretation (Genesis
41:9-13). Pharaoh later found out that this young man was graced with
just the right skills to help save the nation from famine.

Pharaoh inquired of Joseph what he should do, and Joseph
essentially wrote his own job description. As Joseph revealed the plan
that God had given him to help save the nation, Pharaoh knew that

Joseph was the only one who could execute that plan. He not only commuted Joseph's prison sentence, but he also promoted him to prime minister of the nation (Genesis 41:37-45).

Keep in mind that Pharaoh did not ask Joseph to lead a national prayer meeting. Pharaoh did not ask Joseph to put on a clergy collar and lead a tarry service for all of the officials. Pharaoh asked Joseph to use his God-given skills to lead a secular undertaking. That alone will preach.

Joseph's gifts and talents were not only appreciated by a secular king, but they were also needed by him. Those talents were needed by the entire nation. When we begin to think in terms of needs, our views change. Just like Joseph, God has graced us with certain gifts that the world needs. The world needs scientists who are saved, the world needs doctors who have been delivered, the world needs lawyers who love God. The world especially needs the creatives, those who have an eye for design and aesthetics, so that they can beautify what has been built.

Jesus was a problem solver, and we should be problem solvers as his representatives. The Gospel that we are called to preach is the very manifestation of problem-solving. We do a disservice to the world and a dishonor to God if we restrict problem-solving to the church. There are problems in science, problems in medicine, and certainly problems in politics and government. Each of those problems is waiting on a spirit-empowered problem solver to represent the ultimate problem solver, Jesus Christ. Take the Gospel outside of the church.

It is critical that we are effective somewhere other than a pulpit.

God wants us to thrive in this great big world that he put us in. That does not mean that we should be like the world. We should never be like the world—we should be different. In fact, it is that difference that allows us to stand out and advance the Kingdom of God.

Prayer: "God, I thank you for the opportunity to thrive in the world that you've placed me in. I recognize that though I am not of this world you have still purposed for me to be successful in it. I pray that you would give me the wisdom and foresight to be effective in whatever I put my hands to. I pray that even those things outside of the church walls, whether academics, business, social justice, or any other endeavor, would all be made successful with my involvement. You said in Deuteronomy 28 that I should be the head and not the tail, above and not beneath, blessed in the city and in the field, in my coming and in my going, a lender and not a borrower. I receive those promises, and claim them in every secular venture that you lead me to. I ask this in Jesus's name. Amen."

Be relevant

But Peter said, "I have no silver or gold, but what I have I give you; in the name of Jesus Christ of Nazareth, stand up and walk."
—Acts 3:6

Daily Bible Reading: Acts 3:1-10

Are there many things worse than a ministry gift that has no relevance? Anyone can grab a microphone and begin preaching, but it takes a yielded individual to have a word that applies to the circumstances of the people who hear it.

When we think about the word of God there is of course the Logos, the written word of God; and then there is Rhema, the spoken word of God. Both are needed together in order to achieve relevance.

Consider the dynamics of our modern world. There is nothing written in the Bible about the internet. Social media and contemporary pop culture don't show up in the Latin Vulgate, and they shouldn't! I recognize that some who read that statement are going to take issue with it and say that the Bible is applicable today, and it absolutely is! That's part of what most of us believe, that the Bible is the inspired and infallible word of God.[6] The Bible's application is never in question.

At the same time, recognize that there is a difference between a circumstance that can be applied to today and the prophetic word of

---

[6] *Official Manual with the Doctrines and Discipline of the Church of God in Christ, 1973* (Memphis, TN: Church of God in Christ, Pub. Board, 1991), 40.

God for today. The latter is what we should seek to be able to deliver as preachers. Our desire should be to deliver timely messages that meet people where they are. In other words, we need to be relevant.

Caution must be given here: God is in favor of common sense! If you are given an opportunity to preach on a major platform, be prayerful, because it is most likely not the time for you to try out your latest theological position or seek to be as edgy and relevant as possible. Notice, however, that I said "most likely," because at the end of the day, you are accountable to the Holy Spirit and your leadership. Pray, seek God, and determine the direction in which you should go.

One story that every preacher should know well is the story of Peter and John as they went up to the temple to pray (Acts 3:1-10). Peter and John were doing their regular three o'clock business, headed to the prayer meeting. One day, while in route, they encountered a lame man, and unbeknownst to the man this day would change his life forever. The man was doing what he did every day, asking for a crutch, for money, just a little bit to get by to the next day. When the man asked Peter and John for some money, Peter let him know that he did not have money to give him, but he said, "In the name of Jesus Christ of Nazareth, rise up and walk" (v. 6). Peter told the man that he had no silver or gold (money), but what he did have he would give him. What Peter and John had was the power of the Holy Spirit given to them through Jesus Christ.

Relevance is only going to come through the Holy Spirit, and by way of Jesus Christ. That's why it's so important to be focused on preaching the Gospel of Jesus Christ, as the Gospel is permanent good news. The Word of God is the launching point for any relevance. Ask God to give you a ministry of relevance. That doesn't mean have a common ministry. Neither does it mean trying to be like the world to reach the world. It means that we should have something fresh that will speak to the hearts of men and women and meet their needs.

Prayer: "God, you gave Peter and the apostles exactly what they needed to be relevant for the needs of the people they encountered. In the same way, I ask that you help me to walk in relevance. Let the words that I deliver meet people where they are. Let my message and ministry have a positive impact in the time and season in which they are displayed. Let my preaching never become dull, but let everyone I minister to receive what they need at that moment. I ask this in Jesus's name. Amen."

Practice

Do your best to present yourself to God as one approved by him, a
worker who has no need to be ashamed, rightly explaining the word
of truth.
—II Timothy 2:15

Daily Bible Reading: II Timothy 2:14-26

Practice is one of those interesting things that everybody has an
opinion about. My favorite basketball player, hall of famer Allen
Iverson, was castigated for a famous rant about the unimportance of
practice. (He was actually annoyed that the media was wasting his press
conference time asking about practice.)[7] Even though he was taken out
of context, Iverson, and the video clip of him ranting about practice,
is still used by the media to highlight the importance of practice.

There is an old adage that says, "Practice makes perfect," and it
does. There is no profession in which practice is not in the regular
regimen of the successful. Lawyers must not only practice their
command of the law, but trial lawyers specifically have to also practice
their presence and performance in front of a judge and jury. Airline
pilots must have at least 1,500 hours of flight experience to obtain an
airline transport pilot license (ATPL).[8] I think the best place to examine

---

[7] *Iverson*, directed by Zatella Beatty (2014; 214 Films), film.
[8] Federal Aviation Administration, "FAA Boosts Aviation Safety with New Pilot
Qualification Standards," news release, July 10, 2013, Federal Aviation
Administration, accessed December 1, 2017,
https://www.faa.gov/news/press_releases/news_story.cfm?newsId=14838.

practice is sports, in which the greatest athletes in the world are known to spend hours practicing.

The dictionary says that *practice* is "a repeated exercise in or performance of an activity or skill so as to acquire or maintain proficiency in it." As a verb, *practice* is "the act of performing or exercising a skill repeatedly in order to improve." The goal of practice is to improve.[9]

There is no way to get better without practice, and the right way to practice is not to practice on God's people, it's to practice on our own time.

When in doubt, the old fashion way still works. As young preachers, we have to figure out how to practice. If nothing else, buy a mirror, or find a vanity. Use a remote and make it a microphone. Tape-record yourself, time yourself, spend hours doing in private what you want to be successful doing in public. Practice.

In his final words and letter to his protégé Timothy, the Apostle Paul delivered a message that is most often used when talking about study. But I believe this message connects to the idea of practice. Paul told his mentee Timothy, that he should study so that he could be approved by God (II Timothy 2:15). Paul wanted Timothy to recognize that his responsibility was to God much more than to man. Timothy needed to know that his studying wasn't for his glorification, but for the glorification of the God who had commissioned him in the first place.

Ultimately, whatever we do in front of God's people is for God. Practice will lead to the ability to deliver the word more effectively. When we practice, we are less likely to find a reason to be ashamed of our performance. I have found that there is a positive correlation between the amount of time I've spent in preaching practice and my confidence and effectiveness in the pulpit.

Ask God to give you the spirit of practice. Ask God to ignite within you a desire to perfect your craft. Enjoy preaching in the moment, but recognized that you will always have room to grow.

---

9 *Oxford Dictionaries*, s.v. "Practice," accessed December 1, 2017, https://en.oxforddictionaries.com/definition/practice.

Practice doesn't stop with an increase in age—quite the opposite. We must continue to practice. Therefore, work to memorize manuscripts or outlines. The more we practice, the more we will be able to leave notes aside and make eye contact with God's people. All of these things come from practice. There is never a need to be ashamed when we know we rightly performed our duties.

Prayer: "God, help me to perfect the gift that I have. Help me to be dynamic in preaching. Strengthen me to endure practice, even repetition. Help me to strive to memorize messages, and to never be married to a manuscript. Help me to work on my enunciation, my dictation, and my presentation, and to never allow my flesh to take glory from the Gospel. I ask this in Jesus's name. Amen."

Be bold

But Peter and the apostles answered, "We must obey God rather than any human authority. The God of our ancestors raised up Jesus, whom you had killed by hanging him on a tree. God exalted him at his right hand as Leader and Savior that he might give repentance to Israel and forgiveness of sins. And we are witnesses to these things, and so is the Holy Spirit whom God has given to those who obey him."
—Acts 5:29-32

Daily Bible Reading: Acts 5:17-32

One of the enemy's special tools in his toolkit is intimidation. The enemy loves to intimidate people. We, however, make the mistake of thinking that intimidation is always external. Sometimes the worst intimidation comes from within.

This piece of advice is tricky, because it involves balance. You have already been given the advice to remain humble, but here on day 18 the instruction is to be bold. At first thought those may seem like contradictory suggestions, but let me assure you, they are not. There is a reason that God called us to preach. There is a particular way that he formed us, and special gifts and talents that come with our ministry that don't necessarily come with others. That's why we should have confidence in our ability to boldly proclaim the word of God.

Be bold in your local church, but also be bold in your community. The key is to always keep things in perspective. When we are under godly leadership that is appointed to our life, our leader(s) is able to sanction our stepping out on faith. At the end of the day, the most important person to obey is God, but remember he gives us human leadership to follow as well. The more time we spend with God, and the more we learn to hear from him, the more we are able to follow his promptings and directions, and the more successful we become.

It is recorded and the 5th chapter of Acts, how the apostles were persecuted for following God's instructions. The more they preached and taught, the more they were persecuted by the governing authorities. It did not help their case that they were effective in what they did. They likely would have incurred less opposition if they were ineffective—that too will preach. When the Holy Spirit is operating in our work, we're going to be successful at what we do, and the powers of hell are not going to like it. However, know that we don't have to be fooled by intimidation tactics, just as Peter and the apostles were not fooled. When the message came from the authorities, saying, "You were given strict orders not to teach in that name, yet you continue to do it anyway," Peter and his crew answered, "We must obey God rather than any human authority" (vv. 28-29). They went on to remind the governing authorities that Jesus was raised up and exalted. They stood on the Gospel.

When we face opposition, we should remember that Jesus is at the center of it all. There is an Israel Houghton song that says, "Jesus at the center of it all…from beginning to the end, it will always be, it's always been you Jesus." Indeed, it has always been Jesus at the center, which is why we should take confidence in preaching in his name. As preachers, we should strive to keep Jesus at the center of the message we proclaim.

The way to boldness in our preaching ministry is to remember that Jesus was the boldest light to ever shine on the Earth. He shone so bright that sin couldn't stand against him. In his name, the early church operated in boldness, and endured the persecution that came with it. Pray to God to enable you to be bold in your ministry. There will likely be times when as a preacher you are called upon to do non-preaching things. Study, learn, and prepare as much as you can for these assignments.

It may be the laying on of hands, it may be praying for the sick, it may be casting out devils. Whatever it is, it will require boldness that is backed up by the Holy Spirit. Obey God; he won't lead you in the wrong direction.

Prayer: "God, I thank you for holy boldness. Help me to act in wisdom and boldness, even in the face of intimidating powers. You said in your word that I can do all things through Christ who is my strength. Help me in Christ to stand and boldly proclaim the Gospel of Jesus Christ, regardless of the opposition I may face, be it opposition in me or around me. I pray against the spirit of intimidation, for you have not given me the spirit of fear, but of power, and of love, and of sound mind. I thank you for boldness, in Jesus's name. Amen."

Be a servant

I am now rejoicing in my sufferings for your sake, and in my flesh I am completing what is lacking in Christ's afflictions for the sake of his body, that is, the church. I became its servant according to God's commission that was given to me for you, to make the word of God fully known, the mystery that has been hidden throughout the ages and generations but has now been revealed to his saints.
—Colossians 1:24-26

Daily Bible Reading: Colossians 1:24-29; Mark 9:33-37

Never forget that as young preachers our obligation is to serve. Never forget that for any preacher, the obligation is always to serve.

Most of us, if we are honest with ourselves, can admit a certain glorification of microphones. Even preachers who struggle with nervousness (struggling is different than experiencing—we should always experience a little nervousness about preaching) would probably admit that they sometimes place too much focus on the microphone. In many ways, studying, preparing, and delivering the word of God is a form of service. But the average preacher doesn't spend most of their time preaching, and as young preachers, we spend much more time not preaching than we do preaching. Ultimately, how we spend that time in the beginning of our ministry has a major impact on the overall effectiveness of our ministry.

As young preachers, it's important that we find ways to be servants, and always remember that we are called to service. Paul wrote to the

Colossians about his suffering. We know from the life of Paul that he spent a lot of time suffering. He was not suffering randomly either; he was suffering for the cause of the Gospel. Paul's suffering was part of his service. He told the Colossians that his suffering was for their sake. In other words, his service was for their sake, the sake of the people he was called to.

If we really love the people that we preach to—which is a must— we must be willing to think of ourselves as servants to them. Remember that servitude does not mean slavery, and we are not called to be slaves to others, or to allow others to take advantage of us. When we allow others to take advantage of us we are actually being poor stewards of the life and ministry God has given us.

Servant-leadership is about our mindset. We must first think of ourselves as servants. It is recorded several times in the Gospels how Jesus's disciples argued amongst themselves about who was the greatest of the group. Then, when Jesus got around to asking them what they were arguing about, like siblings who had just fought, they were all silent. For those reading who have siblings, this situation probably sounds familiar. Being the all-knowing son of God that Jesus was, he knew that there had been a debate about ranking and positioning. Jesus settled the debate by telling them, "Whoever wants to be first must be last of all and servant of all" (Mark 9:35). The emphasis should be on the word *service*.

Ask God to show you how to serve. He will easily open your eyes to opportunities. People are more likely to embrace the word you attempt to preach to them, if they understand that you are willing to serve them.

Prayer: "God, in my excitement to preach the word, help me to never forget that you have called me to serve. You said that if I want to lead I must first serve. Help me to recognize that the calling on my life is to service. Help me to never preach beyond my ability to serve. Help me to find opportunities to serve your people even in proclaiming the Gospel to them. I ask this in Jesus's name. Amen."

Learn to hear God's voice

Now the LORD came and stood there, calling as before, "Samuel!
Samuel!" And Samuel said, "Speak, for your servant is listening."
—I Samuel 3:10

Daily Bible Reading: I Samuel 3

Be not deceived, God does speak, and as young preachers, we can set ourselves up for a dynamic ministry by learning how to hear his voice.

Here again, a balanced approach is necessary. It is not likely that you'll audibly hear the voice of God every day. For most humans, that is an indication of other issues. Yet, we have to acknowledge that God does speak, and, yes, sometimes he speaks in an audible voice.

After all, the fact that we accepted a call to the preaching ministry means that we believe God called us. This is a great time to pause and ask, how did he call me? How did I know he was calling me? Chances are that you believe that you've heard God's voice at one time or another, either audibly or by way of the Holy Spirit's prompting. It is one thing to acknowledge that he has called us to a particular ministry; it is another thing to become so skilled at hearing his voice that we are able to grow and thrive off of his direction.

I think the best story in the Bible of a young person hearing the voice of God is the story of Samuel. Samuel's very birth was the product of a miracle. Samuel's mother, Hannah, had struggled with infertility for some time, and when God finally gave her a child, she dedicated him back to the service of the Lord (1 Samuel 1:24). Samuel was raised in the temple under the tutelage of the priest Eli. Around the age of twelve, Samuel heard a voice calling him, but did not know that the voice was the voice of God.

I've always found it interesting that Samuel was about twelve years old when this happened. I know from experience as a middle school teacher that puberty happens around that time, and innocent children who used to listen very well and follow directions without difficulty, all of a sudden become hormonal preteens who sometimes struggle to comply with directions. I don't think it was by coincidence that the God who had done little talking for some time—the Bible says the word of the Lord was rare in those days (I Samuel 3:1)—chose a consecrated twelve-year-old to reignite the channels of communication.

Interestingly enough, the text of this story says that Samuel did not yet know the Lord, and the word of the Lord had not yet been revealed to him (v. 7). When God called for the third time, Eli recognized that it was the Lord calling, and told Samuel to say, "Speak, for your servant is listening" (vv. 9-10). Samuel did as he was directed. When the Lord called again, Samuel gave God the acknowledgment that he heard his voice, and God initiated a lifetime of speaking to Samuel. Samuel went on to be the prophet who anointed Israel's first king. Samuel went on to be the prophet who went to Jessie's house in the town of Bethlehem, and found David out in the field, the youngest of his eight brothers, and anointed him as the first king's successor.

It all started with hearing the voice of God.

Remember, though, the Bible says, "The word of the Lord was rare in those days," but immediately after it says, "And there was no widespread revelation." We will never be able to receive the revelation that comes from hearing God's voice if we don't understand the language through which he communicates—his word.

We speak and communicate in English; God speaks and communicates via his word. Strive to be able to recognize God's promptings and directions. Ask God to help you hear him speak.

Prayer: "God, you called out to Samuel in his youth even as he laid on his bed. Your word declares that it is faith that comes by hearing, and that hearing comes by the word of God. As I immerse myself in your word, which is your language, help me to know and recognize your voice. You said that your sheep know your voice, and it is your voice that I need to be an effective preacher. Teach me how to hear you calling, to hear your directions, and to understand your guidance. I ask this in Jesus's name. Amen."

Rely on the Holy Ghost

"But you will receive power when the Holy Spirit has come upon you; and you will be my witnesses in Jerusalem, in all Judea and Samaria, and to the ends of the earth."
—Acts 1:8

Daily Bible Reading: Acts 1:1-11

The advice for day 21 is to rely on the Holy Ghost. There is no substitute for the Holy Ghost, which is not some mysterious, spooky, ethereal mist that floats back and forth like the Force in Star Wars. The Holy Ghost is a co-equal unit of the godhead. The Holy Ghost dwells in believers, and we not only need to be baptized in it, but we also need to rely on it as preachers.

There is a great hymn of the church, written by Frank Bottome in 1890, titled, "The Comforter Has Come." The chorus of the song says, "The comforter has come…The Holy Ghost from Heaven, the father's promise given; Oh, spread the tidings round, wherever man is found—the comforter has come!" Indeed, the Holy Ghost is our comforter, our guide, our leading, and our power. The last thing one should want to be is a powerless preacher. Every time we mount the pulpit, we should want our words to have authority—power.

Pay close attention to the advice given for today—rely on the Holy Ghost. To rely on something means that we depend on it. The word *rely* implies a certain amount of confidence. We can depend on someone or something without ever having confidence in it, but when we rely on something we have an expectation attached to our emotion.

The Holy Ghost is foolproof. It does not and cannot fail. If we are to be effective as young preachers, we must learn to rely on the Holy Ghost.

After his crucifixion, and before his ascension into Heaven, Jesus gave some important instructions to those who would become the first members of his church. Jesus foretold of the baptism of the Holy Ghost (fulfilled in Acts 2), which happened a few days after he delivered those words. But he also told them that they would receive power after the Holy Ghost had come upon them, and that power would enable them to be witnesses (Acts 1:8). What is preaching if it is not witnessing?

One of the most dynamic African-American spiritual leaders of the 20th century was Church of God in Christ (COGIC) founder Bishop C. H. Mason. Mason's life and ministry took a dramatic turn after his encounter with the Holy Ghost at the Azusa Street revival in Los Angeles, California. Mason's ministry became more impactful, and his spiritual gifts changed lives all across the nation. COGIC pioneer and historian Bishop Ithiel C. Clemmons wrote, "Mason began to use his spiritual gifts in his public ministry. He drew large audiences of blacks and whites. wherever he preached, hundreds—and at times up to ten thousand—gathered to hear and receive ministry in outdoor camp meetings."[10] Too often as preachers we try to draw souls with our own power, but Bishop Mason learned that it was the Holy Ghost operating in him that would do the drawing. We would do well to remember the same.

Still, we must never forget that our primary witness is still our life. While lives do not preach, they do testify, and offer evidence of the power of what is being preached. The preaching moment has always been and will always be a powerful opportunity to witness the word of God verbally. If we want to be effective in preaching, if we want to

---

[10] Ithiel C. Clemmons, *Bishop C. H. Mason and the Roots of the Church of God in Christ* (Bakersfield, CA: Pneuma Life, 1996), 63.

have power every time we stand at the sacred desk, we must learn to rely on the Holy Ghost.

Ask God to baptize you in it. It's about more than tongues; it's about empowerment. The baptism in the Holy Ghost is a crisis experience that all believers are entitled to. Ask for it, wait for, and rely upon it.

Prayer: "God, your word says that you have provided for me the Holy Ghost as my helper, to lead me and guide me into all truth. I pray now that you would give me a reliance upon the Holy Ghost. Help me to operate in the power of the power that you sent for my benefit. Help me to utilize the Holy Ghost to be an effective witness, not only where I am, but wherever I go. Help me to learn how to tarry for the Holy Ghost, and how to recognize its authentic presence. Help me to operate and flow in it, and to know it as a personal advocate in my ministry. I ask this in Jesus's name. Amen."

Be self-aware

But he said to me, "My grace is sufficient for you, for my power is made perfect in weakness." Therefore, I will boast all the more gladly about my weaknesses, so that Christ's power may rest on me.
—II Corinthians 12:9, NIV

Daily Bible Reading: II Corinthians 12:1-10

It is to your benefit to be self-aware, but a prerequisite of self-awareness is honesty.

It's near impossible for a preacher of the Gospel to deliver God's truth, if he or she is not truthful with themselves. The truth is, we are flawed individuals. There are things about us that are imperfect, things about us that are somewhat distracting, and things about us that can turn people off from the Gospel if we leave them unchecked.

We never want the word that we preach to be hidden behind our issues. It is important as a young preacher that we understand ourselves. It's beneficial to spend meaningful time reflecting on who we are. We should take feedback when people give it to us, even though it is not always easy to receive. It is actually written in scripture that "faithful are the wounds of a friend" (Proverbs 27:6, KJV).

In his second letter to the Corinthians, Paul got into a little discourse about his weaknesses. He described a challenge that he called an *issue* (or *thorn*) *of the flesh* (II Corinthians 12:7). None of us can know for sure just what that issue was, but we know that it was something that was a weakness for Paul. The word describes Paul asking three times for God to remove that issue from him, but God's response was effectively, "I'm not going to do that. My grace is sufficient for you, and power is made perfect in weakness" (II Corinthians 12:9).

There is a little bit of debate as to just what God meant when he said that. It could've been that God was saying that Paul was okay, even with his weakness; but there are others who believe that God was telling Paul that he had given him the grace to overcome that weakness. I tend to align myself with the second school of thought, articulated often by those like Dr. Matthew L. Stevenson. Regardless, our weaknesses are not there just to be there. They're there to be overcome. In fact, God can get the glory out of our weaknesses.

Consider the first real leader of God's church after Jesus: the Apostle Peter. Peter had been the loudest apostle throughout Jesus's earthly ministry. Peter was easily the most brash in the bunch, and the one quickest to speak up and offer his opinion. Peter was the one ready to curse, the one ready to take up arms and defend what he considered to be right. For most people, Peter's tendency to get ahead of himself was a flaw, and it was. Yet after the founding of the church, what was at one time a flaw for Peter turned out to be a benefit, as he led the church and preached the Gospel helping thousands of souls to come to Christ.

Just like Peter, we are flawed, but that doesn't mean that we should be content with our flaws, nor does it mean that we should be defeated by them. We just need to be self-aware.

Pray that God continues to allow self-awareness to be a part of your ministry. Ask him to reveal to you your flaws, so that you will know those things that need his power. Don't focus on your flaws; just be aware of them, and know that God will always be bigger than them.

Prayer: "God, you made me, my flaws and all. Help me to understand those parts of me that are less than desirable. Help me to be aware of my failings, my weaknesses, my distractions, and my proclivities. Allow me to turn my weaknesses into strengths, and to know that your grace is sufficient to help me overcome them. Help me to never be so consumed with confidence that I forget the parts of me that still need work. I thank you for self-awareness, in Jesus's name. Amen."

Be true to the Gospel of Jesus Christ

But we preach Christ crucified, unto the Jews a stumbling block, and
unto the Greeks foolishness;
But unto them which are called, both Jews and Greeks, Christ the
power of God, and the wisdom of God.
—I Corinthians 1:23-24, KJV

Daily Bible Reading: I Corinthians 1:18-31

It is ever so tempting to want to move a crowd. I don't know many
preachers who like an unengaged congregation. There are times when
we are tempted to say things in a preaching moment to get a particular
reaction. Although this is a natural temptation, it should be overcome,
because one of the most basic things that we need to do as a preacher
is be true to the Gospel of Jesus Christ.

Consider this: no one can preach beyond their position or
experience. However, when we preach, the Gospel we deliver comes
through our lives, and it should be reflective of our lives and our
experience—that's what makes our preaching authentic. Yet, there is a
problem if the message of Jesus Christ is not evident in what we are
preaching.

Please understand, not every message is going to be explicitly
focused on Jesus Christ, and that is okay. Out of ignorance, many try
to say things like, "A preacher should take 'em to the cross every time
they preach." That sounds good in theory, but it's simply not reality,
and some of us would argue that it's not right.

Imagine being given the task of preaching at a youth service, which you may have already experienced. What if the Holy Spirit lets you know that this particular group of young people need to hear a word about not bowing down to pressure. The Holy Spirit may direct to you to preach from the story of the three Hebrew boys in the fiery furnace, allowing you to encourage the young people to stand firm in their faith, and that God will support them in that endeavor. It would be poor preaching practice to all of a sudden try to insert a random exhortation about the cross when preaching from the text about Shadrach, Meshach, and Abednego in Daniel 3.

To be true to the Gospel of Jesus Christ means that the message of Jesus Christ—that is, the good news that delivers, sets captives free, and heals—should be reflected in whatever we're preaching. No, it will not always be a Jesus-specific text. It is not uncommon for many young preachers to begin their ministries with a heavy reliance on Old Testament texts, as the Old Testament is full of stories that lend themselves to manageable sermons.

I would imagine there are very few seasoned pastors who can say they've never preached a Joseph message or a David message. Reality is, both of those figures are key to the story of Jesus. Without Joseph's elevation to prime minister in Egypt, the children of Israel would never have been saved from famine, and the lineage that produced Jesus would've been cut off well before the forty-second generation in which he was born. We're also told of the lineage of Jesus through David's line, and we even find him being called "the son of David" (Matthew 1:1).

Paul brings this message home as he describes how the message of the cross seems foolish to those who are blinded by the world (I Corinthians 1:18). Paul goes on to describe how the Jews of the time were looking for signs of the Messiah, and the Greeks were proud of their philosophy and wisdom, but the Christians stood on the Gospel of Jesus Christ and the fact that he was crucified. That is what they preached. Not only is Christ the power of God, but he is also the wisdom of God.

There are many people who study all they can and still don't understand how the Gospel works. That's the miracle of our faith: one man died to save the entire world from their sins. He lived a perfect life, and demonstrated that we too can walk in God's grace here on earth, denying our flesh in this life. That is the Gospel that we preach: Jesus born, Jesus perfect in living, Jesus crucified, Jesus resurrected, and Jesus presently seated at the right hand of God.

Whatever you do, make sure you preach the true, unadulterated Gospel of Jesus Christ.

Prayer: "God, I recognize the challenges of the times we are living in, and I thank you for giving me a strong foundation in your word. I ask you to give me the courage to boldly proclaim the Gospel of Jesus Christ, and to never waver in doctrine. Help me to be faithful to the text, using the wisdom and guidance of your Holy Spirit. Help me to preach the Gospel when it's popular, preach the Gospel when it's unpopular, and preach the Gospel in the midst of confusion. Let the Gospel of Jesus Christ always be at the center of the word I deliver. I ask this in Jesus's name. Amen."

Be accountable to a pastor

Have confidence in your leaders and submit to their authority,
because they keep watch over you as those who must give an
account. Do this so that their work will be a joy, not a burden, for
that would be of no benefit to you.
—Hebrews 13:17, NIV

Daily Bible Reading: Hebrews 13:1-19

There is a reason God gave us pastors: we need them. As young
preachers, we must be accountable to a pastor. It is possible that your
pastor gave you this devotional, which would indicate that you have a
pastor—that's a great first step. Yet, having a pastor does not indicate
that you are accountable to that pastor. That can only be determined
by your attitude and actions.

Accountability gets a bad rap. It's something that people don't like
to embrace. Our attitude as young preachers should be the opposite.
We should not only embrace accountability, but we should also seek it
out.

Why should we have to make mistakes that could easily be avoided
with the oversight and counsel of a spiritual leader? The job of the
pastor is to watch over souls. Preacher or not, we each have a soul, and
it needs watching. Our ministries also need watching, and as preachers,
especially ones who may be preparing for pastoral ministry someday,
we need a check of accountability over our lives—that's right, lives!
Our preaching ministry does not prevent us from making mistakes,

nor does it keep us from wandering. An accountability system can help to ensure that we do not go wayward, either in our personal Christian walk or in our preaching.

The book of Hebrews is essentially a letter about the priesthood of Jesus Christ. Jesus, the one who should be the focus of our preaching and the one who's name we preach in, is our intercessor. In Romans, Paul indicates that even now Jesus is at the right hand of the father interceding for us (Romans 8:34). I love thinking about that fact, but while it's great to know that Jesus is making intercession for us in Heaven, it's also good to know that God has provided for us human intercessors here on Earth. Chief among those intercessors should be our pastor.

Some of us have been raised in or introduced to hierarchical structures that often emphasize leadership. When there are ranks and tiers of leaders it is not uncommon for there to be an emphasis on obeying leadership. This is apparent outside of the church as well. Consider the military, where obeying the rules of the hierarchy is emphasized. In fact, thinking militaristically has many benefits for us, since our service as preachers is part of a spiritual battle. *The Art of War*, one of the most famous military strategy books of all time, was written by the ancient Chinese strategist Sun Tzu in the fifth century BC. Sun said, "The victories of good warriors are not noted for cleverness or bravery . . . Their victories are not flukes because they position themselves where they will surely win."[11] Warriors need leadership and oversight. Pastors give us both, not as soldiers with arms, but as those who are enlisted in God's service.

As for Hebrews, we don't know for sure who wrote it, but we do know that the writer wants us to obey leadership. He says in the 13th chapter, "Obey your leaders and submit to them, for they are keeping watch over your souls and will give an account. Let them do this with joy and not with sighing" (Hebrews 13:17). Not only should we seek accountability from a pastor, but we should also seek to be a joy to them as they hold us accountable. Our pastor should get fulfillment out of watching us progress and implement the things he or she

---

[11] Sun Tzu, *The Art of War*, trans. Thomas Cleary (Boston: Shambhala, 2017), 62.

teaches us. We should never want to be a burden to our leaders, but should allow them to guide us with joy, and not with stress.

Ask God to help you be a joy to your pastor. Sometimes we seek to get ahead of ourselves, and it certainly takes practice to learn how to submit. The Holy Spirit will help you submit, and in doing so, open you up to the accountability that can help you be successful. Similarly, ask the Holy Spirit to keep you under a godly pastor. Ask God to help you have confidence in the leadership you are assigned to. God will do it.

Prayer: "God, you know my tendency to sometimes get ahead of myself. I thank you for giving me godly leadership to submit to. I ask that you help me to submit, even when my flesh would tell me to do otherwise. Give me confidence in the leadership that you've assigned me to, and the word of God in them. Help me to submit to them, and give them the wisdom to successfully watch out for my soul and steward my development. Help me to be a joy to my leadership and not a burden. I ask this in Jesus's name. Amen."

Never ask to preach

A man's gift maketh room for him, and bringeth him before great
men.
—Proverbs 18:16, KJV

Daily Bible Reading: Proverbs 18

It will be tempting, and you may feel the urge to do so, but never ask
to preach.

There are times when we feel extra confident, when we desire an
opportunity, and there are certainly moments when we feel like we are
the right voice for a particular platform. Still, we need to avoid the
temptation to ask to preach.

The advice for day 25 should not be over-spiritualized. Simply put,
asking to preach is tacky. Even beyond the blatant display of a lack of
patience, asking to preach implies that we think someone not asking
us to preach is an oversight.

Also, please don't confuse the suggestion with what should be done
when opportunities arise in which others put out requests for ministry
gifts. For example, there are times when one is somewhere, maybe a
conference, and the coordinator of a service or program asks if there
is anyone who would like to share a word. Although many of us are
not a fan of that practice either, that is a realistic opportunity that may
arise, and it may be a platform for your exposure. Similarly, there are
times when emergencies or unexpected events happen, and someone
who was slated to be on a program might not show up. In that instance,

you might be in a position to fill in with a sermonette, youthful expressions, or even a full message. Still, it's in our best interest to recognize the difference between asking, and being available.

Under normal circumstances, we're given opportunities in accordance with our effectiveness and God's timing, not because we asked.

Unfortunately, Proverbs 18:16 is one of the most misunderstood scriptures that the church quotes on a regular basis. Indeed, the writer did want us to know that gifts have the power to make room for us, but make no mistake, the writer was not talking about gifts as in talents. The Hebrew word used here is *mattan*, meaning "gifts, offerings, or presents."[12] This scripture is not saying that a special ability to play the organ will make room for us; neither is it talking about a special ability to preach the Gospel, or to sing solos. The writer was saying that when one brings a tangible gift, it will open up access, and bring him or her before great people. A very clear way to see this in practice is politics. Usually, the more money someone donates to a campaign, the more access they get to the candidate. That may seem like a shady practice, but quite frankly, it's really a biblical principle.

How, then, given the real meaning of the scripture, does it apply to the discussion of asking to preach? It applies, because more than asking to preach, one should seek to give. If we really want opportunities to preach, we must learn how to give. As young preachers, we should also be young tithe payers and young offering givers. This too is a general biblical principle, sowing and reaping.

The more seeds we sow into good ground—practical, tangible seeds—the more we stand to benefit. We should never desire to preach more than we desire to give. I know that may sound uncomfortable, but it matters. Our pastors expect us to give, and we should want to give. Someday many of you will be pastoring, if you're not already, and when you're in that position, the last thing you're going to want is an ambitious young preacher who doesn't support the ministry with their substance. The Bible says that God gives seed to the sower. Ask God

---

[12] *Blue Letter Bible*, "Proverbs 18:16 (KJV)," accessed December 1, 2017, https://www.blueletterbible.org/kjv/pro/18/16/t_conc_646016.

to help you give. The more you give tangible gifts, the more doors will open for your talents.

Prayer: "God, you see the zeal and enthusiasm I have for preaching. You also see my nervousness. Help me to trust that doors for preaching will be opened for me at the right times, and teach me how to give more than I expect to receive. Give me the spirit of giving, of myself, of my time, and my talents, trusting that you will return for me opportunities to share your word. I ask this in Jesus's name. Amen."

Learn the discipline of consecration

And he said unto them, This kind can come forth by nothing, but by
prayer and fasting.
—Mark 9:29, KJV

Daily Bible Reading: Mark 9:14-29; Matthew 6:1-18

Notice that the advice for today is to learn the discipline of
consecration, because indeed, consecration is a discipline.

This is one of the tricky parts for young preachers. If you are on
the younger end, meaning closer to or still a teenager, you might still
be in high school. If you're in your teens you probably have regular
activities like sports, and other parts of youth that immerse you in the
culture. If you are on the older end of the younger preachers, you might
just be starting your professional career, and that can bring its own set
of challenges. Regardless, you must embrace the discipline of
consecration.

Too often Christians confuse consecration with spookiness. The
Bible never presents consecration as spookiness, but it does require
the ability to separate. We know that it's important, because in the Old
Testament when Moses consecrated the priestly officers, the officers
were instructed to remain separate for seven days (Leviticus 8). Their
literal separation helped to provide a figurative separation from the
world they were called to minister before.

In the New Testament, in Mark's Gospel, we read about how
Jesus's disciples were unable to cast out an unclean spirit, primarily

because they lacked the strength that comes from consecration. When they asked Jesus why they were not able to cast out the spirit, Jesus replied: "This kind only comes out with prayer," and several versions add, "and fasting" (Mark 9:29).

In Matthew's Gospel, we read of the famous Sermon on the Mount, in which Jesus gave us some of the most important instructions for Christian living we have. Here Jesus outlines the three elements of consecration: praying, fasting, and giving. Regarding each of these, Jesus is very clear, they are to be done in secret, so that God can recognize them openly (Matthew 6:1-18). Jesus was teaching this against the backdrop of religious individuals who were doing these things for the praise and admiration of people, and not for the glorification of God.

Most of the time when we think about consecration, we immediately go to praying and fasting, but we must also remember that giving is a part of consecration as well. Each of these actions demonstrates our faith in God and reliance upon him. When we pray, we speak to a God who we cannot see, but our faith tells us that he hears us and will answer us. Our fasting is literal denial of our flesh, and we do it in the faith that God will feed us spiritually. When we give of our substance, we trust that we are investing it in God's work, and that he will repay at the right time and in the right manner. Each of these is a critical element of consecration, and together, they can help move us closer to God's presence.

So much can be said about how to do these things, but the simple message is that it's in our best interest as preachers to learn how to consecrate. While true fasting is denial of food, there are times when we have to fast from non-edible things. There are times when we are not able to watch our favorite shows on television or engage in certain conversations. The key is to replace the denied activity with attention and focus on God.

Instead of reading information on social media, we should take the time to read the word of God. Instead of eating our favorite meal, or regular snacks, we should take the opportunity to draw closer to God. We can only be as powerful as our ability to consecrate.

Ask God to show you how he would want you to separate yourself for ministry, and ask him for his assistance in doing so.

Prayer: "God, I need power to preach, but I can only get it in time spent with you. Teach me the discipline of consecration. Help me to withdraw when my flesh wants me to hang around. Help me to deny myself when my flesh wants me to indulge. Show me how to continually present my body a living sacrifice, so that you can renew my mind for my assignment. Help me to regularly turn my plate down, and to separate for a season when necessary. Let my consecration be about more of you—through praying, and fasting, and giving—and not about me. I ask this in Jesus's name. Amen."

Love people

And now faith, hope, and love abide, these three; and the greatest of
these is love.
—I Corinthians 13:13

Daily Bible Reading: I Corinthians 13; John 3:16

This should be an obvious suggestion, but unfortunately it is not. Far
too many preachers love microphones more than they love God's
people. Every once in a while, it's good to pause and ask ourselves,
why do I preach? Obvious immediate answers are, because God called
me, or because I was gifted with an ability to speak. Also among those
answers should be, because of my love for God's people.

None of us can effectively minister to people we do not love. An
easy way to keep this in perspective is to think about the unlovable
parts of our own natures. As we stop to reflect, we come to realize that
there is a lot about each of us that is seemingly unlovable. There are
undesirable attributes that we all have. For one it may be arrogance,
for another pride, and others lack forgiveness; but even in our
preaching selves, we have things that God does not like. Yet, his grace
allows us to be used in spite of those things. If God loves us in spite
of our imperfections, how much more should we love his people?

The scripture that is probably referenced most when speaking
about love is the 13th chapter of First Corinthians. In this chapter, Paul
writes to the Corinthians about the nature of love. He says that all of
the speaking in tongues and all of the prophetic power and knowledge

is meaningless if he does not love. Paul goes on to describe love as patient and kind, not boastful or rude. Paul even goes on to say that love does not end; after all, how could it? Elsewhere in scripture, we read that God is love (I John 4:8), and we know that God does not end, so neither should love end. The thing is, we must recognize that as his ministers, we need to be instruments of God's love.

Of course, the full display of God's love is embodied in Jesus Christ. That famous scripture that many of us learn in our youth or early Sunday school days tells us that God so loved the world that he gave his only son, that whoever believes in him (the drunkard, the prostitutes, the gamblers, the liars) might not perish, but receive their access to everlasting life (John 3:16). That is a beautiful thing, and it should come across in our preaching.

Young preachers are typically not pastors. Still, every preacher needs to know that once they become a preacher, they become a leader in the eyes of many people. According to Lora-Ellen McKinney, "The work of church leaders is to provide . . . the tools to make whole all who enter its doors. The most important tool is love; the most important action is the extension of that love to God's people."[13] Many of my early struggles as a church leader were the result of a failure to keep love at the forefront of my words or actions. When I began to think more intentionally about displaying compassion (connected to love), I began to avoid many mistakes.

In our preaching ministries, we should always remember that they should be ministries of love. That is not to say that love doesn't sometimes have to deliver difficult messages. In fact, when we really love people, we're willing to tell the truth, even when it makes us uncomfortable. But there is a way to do that, that is not off-putting and destructive. It is a message of love that brings people to conviction.

That's why children crave discipline. Although a child might not like restrictions in the moment, children understand the destruction that comes when there are no boundaries. They understand discipline

---

[13] Lora-Ellen McKinney, ed. *Total Praise: An Orientation to Black Baptist Belief and Worship* (Valley Forge, Pa: Judson Press, 2003), 78.

is a form of love from their parents and teachers, and even if they don't necessarily like it, they appreciate it.

Our ministry mindset should be a mindset of love, our preaching should be preaching of love, and our heart posture should be one that loves the people God has assigned us to preach to. God loves us, and we must love his people.

Prayer: "God, you love me even though many times I'm unlovable. Thank you for loving me so much that you would give your only son, Jesus, to die for me. Give me the burden of Love for your people—to love them and not just preach to them. Show me how to love them in spite of their flaws, as you love me in spite of mine. Help me to never be so focused on correction that I forget to love. I ask this in Jesus's name. Amen."

Feed the people

How, then, can they call on the one they have not believed in? And how can they believe in the one of whom they have not heard? And how can they hear without someone preaching to them?
—Romans 10:14, NIV

Daily Bible Reading: Romans 10:5-17; John 21:15-17

As preachers of the Gospel, we are servers, waiters and, if you will. We preach to feed the people.

C. Ivan Johnson, the young pastor of the Greater Destiny Church in Tacoma, Washington, told me, "We preach to feed, not to fulfill our needs." That is a simple yet powerful reflection from a young preacher who has achieved success in ministry even at a relatively young age. Pastor Johnson is supported by scripture, as Jesus told us in Matthew that, "Man shall not live on bread alone, but on every word that comes from the mouth of God" (Matthew 4:4). The point: feed God's people with the word.

As with the other advice given in this devotional, the advice for day 28 may seem like an obvious task for the preacher, but the evidence of it not being obvious is that so many preachers neglect to do it. As young preachers, the sooner we learn to ensure that the people who hear us preach are fed, the more effective we will be in ministry. There is nothing wrong with getting fulfillment from preaching. As a matter of fact, we should be fulfilled in doing what God has called us to do. Most of us find out early on in our preaching ministry that there is a sense of joy and excitement that comes with preaching effectively. When God's spirit moves over us in the preaching moment, we feel a sort of rush, especially when the effectiveness of our ministry has been affirmed via crowd response or the move of the Spirit. Still, we must remember that we are there to feed God's people.

Consider the kid who loves candy. Every time the kid pops candy in her mouth, she is eating. Yet, one is left asking the question, is the little girl really being fed? I would argue that she's not being fed. Sugar-filled candy may satisfy a child's desire in the moment, but it will never fulfill their needs. To be honest, there is something a little creepy about those who only give kids candy. Candy can be good as an occasional treat, but there is nothing about candy that is nutritious in the long term. If anything, candy is full of destructive things. With that in mind, we need to consider our role in feeding God's sheep. Every time we step into a pulpit, we should be delivering a prepared and substantive meal that can feed the people.

Of course, that isn't to say there aren't some times when we'll be put on the spot. Even as a young preacher I've experienced moments when I've needed to give a message on short notice. That's all the more reason to be prepared. Regular study and regular consecration leads to a more constant state of preparation. As preachers, we should always be prepared to do just that: preach.

In the tenth chapter of his letter to the church at Rome, Paul discusses how salvation is for everyone, but he's clear that preachers are important. Paul asked the rhetorical questions, "How can people call on someone they've never believed in? How can they believe in someone they've never heard? How can they hear without someone proclaiming that voice?" Finally, Paul asks, how can someone proclaim that voice if they were not sent by God as his representative? (v. 14). The answer is, they can't. In answering God's call to preach the Gospel, we acknowledged that we believed God sent us to proclaim his word. If we do that, his people will be fed.

Our task is to do what Jesus told Peter to do: feed his sheep. Peter was adamant that he loved Jesus, and each time Peter affirmed his love, Jesus told him to feed or tend to the sheep (John 21:15-17).

Preaching God's word is not necessarily loving God, although we should strive to do both. If as preachers we say we love God, we must feed his sheep.

Prayer: "God, it was you who called me to preach the Gospel; therefore it must be you who feeds me. I ask you to equip me to feed your people with the word of God. I ask for the prophetic revelation that will cause hearts to be full. I ask for wisdom and insight to deliver your word in a way that will be received. I ask that you give me the word that will leave your people always full and never empty. This I ask in Jesus's name. Amen."

Enjoy your youth

Don't let anyone look down on you because you are young, but set
an example for the believers in speech, in conduct, in love, in faith
and in purity.
—I Timothy 4:12, NIV

Daily Bible Reading: I Timothy 4

If one is a young preacher, they should be a young preacher, and enjoy
their youth.

In his book, *The Good Life*, hip-hop artist and Christian Trip Lee,
also a young preacher, cautions against enjoying life in the wrong way.
Lee wrote, "God has given us many things to enjoy, but we must enjoy
them rightly . . . We should enjoy God's gifts, but we shouldn't forget
the One to whom they're pointing us."[14] We are wise to take Mr. Lee's
advice, as there is a right way and a wrong way to enjoy the life God
has given us. Balance is the key. I don't believe that God is glorified by
a life of a preacher that is absent of any fun and enjoyment, especially
during the years that fun and enjoyment should be most accessible.

Unfortunately, many young preachers forget that they are young
and that they are in a time of life that is meant to be enjoyed. Youth
and vitality are not guaranteed for the duration of our lives. In fact, the
Bible hints at the difficulties that come with old age. For that reason,
it is important that we make use of our youth, not only in the church,

---

[14] Trip Lee, *The Good Life* (Chicago: Moody, 2012), 133-134.

but also outside of the church. It is our lives outside of the church that should go the farthest in helping to draw souls to Christ.

Youth is a time of exploration and enjoyment. During youth, we should take the opportunity to do things that we will not be able to do when we are older.

You may be young and unmarried; enjoy that. You may be childless; enjoy that. That is not to say that marriage and having children are not to be desired. They are God-given institutions to advance his Kingdom, and both have their place. The vast majority of humans are not called to the ministry of abstinence, and thus should desire to have a godly marriage and to be godly parents someday. Emphasis on *someday*.

While we wait for those institutions to materialize in our lives, we should embrace the season of life called youth. That means taking the time to see the world as much as possible, taking trips and traveling. It means spending time laughing and joking with friends, and doing the leisurely things that the pressures of life can sometimes make difficult. We can preach and still have fun as young people. In fact, we should, because the appropriate enjoyment of life glorifies God.

In his first letter to Timothy, Paul warns against those who are falsely deep. Depth by itself is not a bad thing, as the opposite of depth is shallowness. God is a deep God, and we should seek to get as much of him as we can. What we should not seek to do is become un-relatable or detached from reality. That is not depth; it's oddness.

Paul also gives Timothy some advice on how to be a good young minister of Jesus Christ. Paul tells Timothy not to let anyone despise his youth, but to be an example of a young person who loves Jesus Christ (I Timothy 4:12). Paul provides four things for Timothy to consider in his youth: his speech and conduct, his love, his faith, and his purity. Striving toward considering those things in a godly manner was the way that Timothy could embrace youth and still be an effective minister. We know this because Paul also told Timothy not to neglect the gifts given to him. The message for us is to embrace our youth, but also not to neglect the gift given to us to preach the Gospel.

Ask God to show you how to achieve this balance. Balance is not just something needed in this instance. Balance is key to being an effective minister of the Gospel. The sooner one learns balance in their life, the stronger they will be as a preacher, and as a citizen of a very real world. Learn balance in your youth, have fun, and minister. These are not opposing actions. They are not mutually exclusive. They all go together, to the glory of God.

Prayer: "God, I thank you for youth and vitality. I thank you that I am in the prime of my life and my best years are ahead of me. Help me to appreciate this stage of life called youth. Help me not to want to age too fast, but allow me to reap the benefits of youth, and to accomplish everything you have for me in this season. I ask this in Jesus's name. Amen."

Avoid the temptation to compare

David strapped Saul's sword over the armor, and he tried in vain to
walk, for he was not used to them. Then David said to Saul, "I
cannot walk with these; for I am not used to them." So David
removed them.
—I Samuel 17:39

Daily Bible Reading: I Samuel 17:34-51

The final piece of advice in our journey sounds like several other pieces
of advice, but is a critical consideration nonetheless: do not fall into
the trap of comparing yourself to others.

The truth is, there are some things that most people do for just a
season of their lives. Think about it: most people work for a certain
amount of time and then retire from their job. No one drives a school
bus forever, and no one teaches forever. Sure, some people pass away
working in these positions, but for the most part, the expectation is
that they will work for a certain amount of time and then retire at the
right time. Preaching is not like that. With little exception, we will be
preaching for the rest of our lives. There may come a time when the
engagements will be fewer and we are traveling less, but as long as God
gives us strength, we will likely be called upon to deliver his word.
Note, I am referring to being available to preach, not to having a
regular preaching obligation, nor to serving as a pastor indefinitely.

Just like we can't compare our jobs to those of other people, we
also can't compare ourselves to other people. One of the easiest ways

to diminish our power is to compare ourselves to others. When we are stuck in comparison, our eyes and our focus are off of Jesus Christ. Comparison cannot happen without some sort of observation. That's what comparison is: identifying how things are similar. Contrasting is identifying how things are different. If we are honest, most of us, particularly those of us in public ministry, have struggled with comparison and contrasting. This problem has been accentuated by technology that now allows us to observe other people instantaneously.

Most things in life have a good side and a bad side. The good thing about technology and preaching is that we can learn from others and be encouraged at times when we seem to be pouring out more than receiving. The bad thing about technology is that we are left comparing ourselves to others, even though God's purposes for our lives are completely different.

The story of David going out to fight Goliath contains a lot of wisdom regarding comparison. Although David was not directly comparing himself to Saul, for a moment, David attempts to go out and fight Goliath in Saul's armor (I Samuel 17:38). The course of history would've been vastly different had David kept on Saul's armor beyond the dressing room that was Saul's court. We read in first Samuel that when David puts on the armor given to him by Saul, he is uncomfortable in it, as he is not used to it, and thus unable to be effective. David realized this early on and wisely rejected the armor. David was a shepherd boy, who was much more skilled with a slingshot and stones.

There have been periods in all of our lives in which we've tried on someone else's armor, hoping to defeat some enemy. But when we use someone else's armor we deny the power of all that God has done in our lives. Saul's armor was the appropriate choice for an arrogant king. Saul's armor was fitting for someone who had already lost their power, as Saul had. Saul's armor was good for someone who had demonstrated that they had difficulty obeying God. However, for a shepherd boy after God's own heart like David, the appropriate weapons and armor were much simpler.

You may already know from Sunday school how the story ends: David defeated Goliath using his own tools. He used the weapons that he knew from time tending sheep and time out in the fields fighting off lions and bears. David viewed Goliath as no different than those animals.

What if David had gotten bogged down in comparing himself to Saul, looking at how Saul's armor fit, and second-guessing why he couldn't maneuver in it like the king? My guess is that David probably would not have defeated Goliath, if for no other reason than the mental anguish he would've been experiencing in comparison.

Unknowingly we do the same thing in our ministries, but all of us must reject this. Our stories are different than others'. David's preparation for battle was different than the king's. Nevertheless, when it was all said and done, it was David and not king Saul who took the giant down.

On this, day 30, the final lesson is, as young preachers, we must never fall into the trap of comparison. We should always remember that what God has for us is for us. Our story and our trajectory matter. We have a responsibility to trust and believe that both will be used for the glory of God.

Prayer: "God, you gave David a special set of tools to accomplish his mission. I believe that you have done the same for me. I ask that you give me the strength to recognize the uniqueness of my journey, and that I'm right where you want me to be. Help me to be comfortable in what you called me to do, and in the way in which you've called me to do it. Help me to avoid the temptation to compare myself to others, but to find my story in yours. I ask this in Jesus's name. Amen."

Afterword

I can do all things through Christ which strengtheneth me.
—Philippians 4:13, KJV

It probably didn't take long for you to realize that there are many other pieces of advice that could've been included in this devotional. That's because it's almost impossible to create an exhaustive list of tips for a young preacher. The changing nature of our world means that every day technology advances, new conversations arise, and unforeseen challenges present themselves. With each passing moment, the realm in which we exist is slightly different than it was the moment before. That's one of the reasons I love the word of God so much. God's word, written and spoken, has proven to be foolproof and consistent even when things seem to be changing. We are reminded in the book of Ecclesiastes that, "What has been is what will be, and what has been done is what will be done; there is nothing new under the sun" (Ecclesiastes 1:9). There is nothing new. Sure, problems dress themselves in different clothes, and challenges adorn themselves with different cologne, but the foundational principles and rules governing our world have stood the same since the beginning of time.

As you continue in your walk, and continue to reflect upon the call to preach, consider how we are each just one dot in God's universe, yet he is concerned about us nonetheless. There are literally billions of individuals on the planet, each of whom has a call and a destiny on their lives, yet God is equally concerned about every one of us fulfilling our individual assignment—I know for me that is a powerful thought.

In fulfilling our assignment, there are always going to be seasons in which our work is made more difficult, especially when there are critical problems in an area God has assigned us to. Think about it, the world still looks to the preacher to be able to offer comforting words when a loved one passes away. Most Christian men and women still want the preacher to affirm their union and present them as husband and wife. Almost all churchgoers want to hear a moving word preached to them on Sunday morning. These are just some of the things that affirm that the preacher is still needed, even in our technologically advancing society.

All of this may make the call to preach seem daunting, but remember, we're not supposed to fulfill the call alone. Paul wrote to the Philippians, "I can do all things through Christ which strengtheneth me" (Philippians 4:13, KJV). Paul did not say that he could do all things through his education; neither did he say he could do all things through his connection with a well-known mentor. Paul wanted the Philippian church to know that the Christ for which he would suffer was the one who would empower him to accomplish everything he was called to. That doesn't mean that we are to forsake the other things. We owe it to ourselves to utilize what God has given us, including access to learning and ministry preparation. The key is to not forget who is the ultimate source of our strength, and the strength of our lives.

Satan despises works like these, those that call God's ministry gifts back to obedience. He can't stand the idea of young men and women being affirmed in their call, not for fame or fortune, but out of love for and obedience to the one who called them. Power in preaching comes when we remember who has all power over Satan. Back in Genesis when Adam and Eve fell, it was said that the deceiving serpent would bruise the heel of someone, but that the someone would crush the serpent's head (Genesis 3:15). Who is the crusher? He is the Christ!

As preachers, everything we do must be about the Christ.

Preach Christ.

About the Author

Kyle J. Boyer is an educator, social justice advocate, and minister. His work and studies lie at the intersection of education, public policy, and theology. A career educator, he has taught at the middle and high school levels, and is an elected member of the Tredyffrin/Easttown Board of School Directors. He serves the community as an Executive Committee member of the West Chester Branch of the NAACP, and as a member of the Advisory Board of the Foundation for Learning in Tredyffrin/Easttown (FLITE). He is an ordained Elder in the Church of God in Christ, and has worked in youth ministry on the local and regional levels. Since 2010, he has been on staff at his lifelong church, the Mt. Carmel Church of God in Christ in West Chester, PA. He serves as the Vice President of the West Chester Ministerial Alliance and is a member of the Main Line Black Interdenominational Ministers Alliance. He is a graduate of the George Washington University and holds master's degrees in education and public administration from the University of Pennsylvania. He is currently completing the Master of Divinity program at United Lutheran Seminary. Boyer resides and works in Chester County, Pennsylvania.